JACULA PRUDENTUM

Jacula
Prudentum

Outlandish Proverbs, Sentences, etc.

SELECTED BY

MR. GEORGE HERBERT

LATE ORATOR OF THE UNIVERSITY OF CAMBRIDGE

MINNEAPOLIS

Published by Curiosmith.
Minneapolis, Minnesota.
Internet: curiosmith.com.

Previously published as: *Outlandish Proverbs, selected by Mr. G.H.* LONDON, PRINTED BY
T. P. FOR HUMPHREY BLUNDEN, AT THE CASTLE IN CORNHILL, 1640.
The second edition: *Jacula Prudentum: or Outlandish Proverbs, Sentences,* &c. Selected
by Mr. George Herbert, late orator of the University of Cambridg. LONDON, PRINTED BY
T. MAXEY FOR T. GARTHWAIT, AT THE LITTLE NORTH DOOR OF ST. PAUL'S, 1651, included
some additions.

Words marked with an asterisk* are defined in the Glossary in the back of the book.
Definitions are from *Webster's 1828 American Dictionary of the English Language, Webster's
1913 Dictionary, or Wiktionary, the free dictionary.*

Scripture quotations designated (NIV) are from the Holy Bible, NEW INTERNATIONAL
VERSION®. Copyright © 1973, 1978, 1984 by Biblica, Inc. All rights reserved worldwide.
Used by permission.

Supplementary content, compilation, book layout, and cover design:
Copyright © 2018 Charles J. Doe

ISBN 9781946145369

CONTENTS

INTRODUCTORY NOTE

Being old and common sayings that briefly and forcibly express truths, as results of experience and observation, proverbs are often expressive of the thoughts of a people or a nation. The editor of Herbert's works says that proverbs formed a favorite study of that age, and were a means of knowing the mind of the several nations to which their authors belonged. The proverbs of Mr. Herbert were first published in a small volume in 1640. So popular were they that a second and enlarged edition was issued in 1651. [Under the quaint but expressive name *Jacula Prudentum*, or Darts of the Wise.] The entire collection is curious and interesting, many of them being condensed rules of life, are worthy of being often read and long remembered.

Some of the better and more practical sayings of SHAKESPEARE have become proverbial, and are quoted not only as indexes of the character of their author and his age, but of human nature, as they are often suited to all ages.

The proverbs of Solomon constitute some of the wisest and truest maxims, as they are eminently suited to practical life in all time. Being short allegorical sayings that contain more meaning than meets the eye or than lies on the surface, they are designed, as the original Hebrew word means, *to govern* the whole conduct of a person.

Our LORD often spoke in parables and taught by allegories. Indeed a profound scholar and critical writer[1] says, "That true Light, which lightens every man that cometh into the world, first taught men to acknowledge Himself as the Fountain and Giver of all good; and then by *short maxims*, conveyed in terse, energetic words, taught them to regulate their conduct in life, in respect to the dispensations of His providence, and in reference to each other in domestic, social, and civil life. The different changes which take place in society; the new relations which in process of time men would bear to each other; the invention in arts and sciences, and the *experience* of those who had particularly considered the ways of the Lord, and marked the operations of his hands, would give rise to many maxims, differing from the original stock only in their application to those *new relations* and *varying circumstances.*"

[BOSTWICK HAWLEY (1814–1910). *Beauties of George Herbert*, 1877.]

---

1 Dr. Adam Clarke.

Jacula Prudentum

OLD men go to death; death comes to young men.

———○○○○○———

MAN proposeth, God disposeth.

———○○○○○———

HE begins to die that quits his desires.

———○○○○○———

A HANDFUL of good life is better then a bushel of learning.

———○○○○○———

HE that studies his content, wants it.

———○○○○○———

EVERY day brings its bread with it.

———○○○○○———

HUMBLE hearts have humble desires.

———○○○○○———

HE that stumbles and falls not, mends his pace.

———○○○○○———

THE house shows the owner.

———o○҉○o———

HE that gets out of debt, grows rich.

———o○҉○o———

ALL is well with him who is beloved of his neighbors.

———o○҉○o———

BUILDING and marrying of children are great wasters.

———o○҉○o———

A GOOD bargain is a pick-purse.

———o○҉○o———

THE scalded dog fears cold water.

———o○҉○o———

PLEASING ware is half sold.

———o○҉○o———

LIGHT burdens, long borne, grow heavy.

———o○҉○o———

THE wolf knows what the ill beast thinks.

———o○҉○o———

WHO has none to still him, may weep out his eyes.

———o○҉○o———

WHEN all sins grow old, covetousness is young.

———o○҉○o———

IF ye would know a knave,* give him a staff.

———o○҉○o———

YOU cannot know wine by the barrel.

———o○҉○o———

A cool mouth and warm feet live long.

————∘ₒ⟨⊙⟩ₒ∘————

A horse made, and a man to make.

————∘ₒ⟨⊙⟩ₒ∘————

Look not for musk in a dog's kennel.

————∘ₒ⟨⊙⟩ₒ∘————

Not a long day, but a good heart, rids work.

————∘ₒ⟨⊙⟩ₒ∘————

He pulls with a long rope that waits for another's death.

————∘ₒ⟨⊙⟩ₒ∘————

Great strokes make not sweet music.

————∘ₒ⟨⊙⟩ₒ∘————

A cask and an ill custom must be broken.

————∘ₒ⟨⊙⟩ₒ∘————

A fat housekeeper makes lean executors.

————∘ₒ⟨⊙⟩ₒ∘————

Empty chambers make foolish maids.

————∘ₒ⟨⊙⟩ₒ∘————

The gentle hawk half-mans* herself.

————∘ₒ⟨⊙⟩ₒ∘————

The Devil is not always at one door.

————∘ₒ⟨⊙⟩ₒ∘————

When a friend asks, there is no tomorrow.

————∘ₒ⟨⊙⟩ₒ∘————

God sends cold according to clothes.

————∘ₒ⟨⊙⟩ₒ∘————

ONE sound blow will serve to undo us all.

———·o·ᖇ·o·———

HE loseth nothing, that loseth not God.

———·o·ᖇ·o·———

THE German's wit is in his fingers.

———·o·ᖇ·o·———

AT dinner my man appears.

———·o·ᖇ·o·———

WHO gives to all, denies all.

———·o·ᖇ·o·———

QUICK believers need broad shoulders.

———·o·ᖇ·o·———

WHO remove stones, bruise their fingers.

———·o·ᖇ·o·———

BENEFITS please like flowers while they are fresh.

———·o·ᖇ·o·———

BETWEEN the business of life and the day of death a space
ought to be interposed.

———·o·ᖇ·o·———

ALL came from, and will go to others.

———·o·ᖇ·o·———

HE that will take the bird, must not scare it.

———·o·ᖇ·o·———

HE lives unsafely that looks too near on things.

———·o·ᖇ·o·———

A GENTLE housewife mars the household.

———◦◦°◎°◦◦———

A CROOKED log makes a straight fire.

———◦◦°◎°◦◦———

HE has great need of a fool that plays the fool himself.

———◦◦°◎°◦◦———

A MERCHANT that gains not, loseth.

———◦◦°◎°◦◦———

LET not him that fears feathers come among wild-fowl.

———◦◦°◎°◦◦———

LOVE and a cough cannot be hid.

———◦◦°◎°◦◦———

A DWARF on a giant's shoulder sees further of the two.

———◦◦°◎°◦◦———

HE that sends a fool means to follow him.

———◦◦°◎°◦◦———

BRABBLING curs never want sore ears.

———◦◦°◎°◦◦———

BETTER the feet slip than the tongue.

———◦◦°◎°◦◦———

FOR washing his hands, none sells his lands.

———◦◦°◎°◦◦———

A LION's skin is never cheap.

———◦◦°◎°◦◦———

THE goat must browse where she is tied.

———◦◦°◎°◦◦———

NOTHING is to be presumed on, or despaired of.

———⸰o⸰❁⸰oo———

WHO has a wolf for his mate, needs a dog for his man.

———⸰o⸰❁⸰oo———

IN a good house all is quickly ready.

———⸰o⸰❁⸰oo———

A BAD dog never sees the wolf.

———⸰o⸰❁⸰oo———

GOD oft has a great share in a little house.

———⸰o⸰❁⸰oo———

ILL ware is never cheap.

———⸰o⸰❁⸰oo———

A CHEERFUL look makes a dish a feast.

———⸰o⸰❁⸰oo———

IF all fools had baubles,* we should want fuel.

———⸰o⸰❁⸰oo———

VIRTUE never grows old.

———⸰o⸰❁⸰oo———

EVENING words are not like to morning.

———⸰o⸰❁⸰oo———

WERE there no fools, bad ware would not pass.

———⸰o⸰❁⸰oo———

NEVER had ill workman good tools.

———⸰o⸰❁⸰oo———

HE stands not surely that never slips.

———⸰o⸰❁⸰oo———

WERE there no hearers, there would be no backbiters.

———◦◦⚬◦◦———

EVERYTHING is of use to a housekeeper.

———◦◦⚬◦◦———

WHEN prayers are done, my lady is ready.

———◦◦⚬◦◦———

CITIES seldom change religion only.

———◦◦⚬◦◦———

AT length the fox turns monk.

———◦◦⚬◦◦———

FLIES are busiest about lean horses.

———◦◦⚬◦◦———

HEARKEN to reason, or she will be heard.

———◦◦⚬◦◦———

THE bird loves her nest.

———◦◦⚬◦◦———

EVERYTHING new is fine.

———◦◦⚬◦◦———

WHEN a dog is a drowning, every one offers him drink.

———◦◦⚬◦◦———

BETTER a bare foot than none.

———◦◦⚬◦◦———

WHO is so deaf as he that will not hear?

———◦◦⚬◦◦———

HE that is warm thinks all so.

———◦◦⚬◦◦———

AT length the fox is brought to the furrier.

———○o┆◎┆o○———

HE that goes barefoot must not plant thorns.

———○o┆◎┆o○———

THEY that are booted are not always ready.

———○o┆◎┆o○———

HE that will learn to pray, let him go to sea.

———○o┆◎┆o○———

IN spending lies the advantage.

———○o┆◎┆o○———

HE that lives well is learned enough.

———○o┆◎┆o○———

ILL vessels seldom miscarry.

———○o┆◎┆o○———

A FULL belly neither fights nor flies well.

———○o┆◎┆o○———

ALL truths are not to be told.

———○o┆◎┆o○———

AN old wise man's shadow is better than a young buzzard's sword.

———○o┆◎┆o○———

NOBLE housekeepers need no doors.

———○o┆◎┆o○———

EVERY ill man has his ill day.

———○o┆◎┆o○———

SLEEP without supping, and wake without owing.

———○o┆◎┆o○———

I GAVE the mouse a hole, and she is become my heir.

———oo⫯o⫯oo———

ASSAIL who will, the valiant attends.

———oo⫯o⫯oo———

WHITHER goest, grief? Where I am wont.

———oo⫯o⫯oo———

PRAISE day at night, and life at the end.

———oo⫯o⫯oo———

WHITHER shall the ox go where he shall not labor?

———oo⫯o⫯oo———

WHERE you think there is bacon, there is no chimney.

———oo⫯o⫯oo———

MEND your clothes, and you may hold out this year.

———oo⫯o⫯oo———

PRESS a stick, and it seems a youth.

———oo⫯o⫯oo———

THE tongue walks where the teeth speed not.

———oo⫯o⫯oo———

A FAIR wife and a frontier castle breed quarrels.

———oo⫯o⫯oo———

LEAVE jesting whiles it pleaseth, lest it turn to earnest.

———oo⫯o⫯oo———

DECEIVE not thy physician, confessor, nor lawyer.

———oo⫯o⫯oo———

ILL natures, the more you ask them, the more they stick.

———oo⫯o⫯oo———

VIRTUE and a trade are the best portion for children.

——o○⦂◉⦂○o——

THE chicken is the country's, but the city eats it.

——o○⦂◉⦂○o——

HE that gives thee a capon, give him the leg and the wing.

——o○⦂◉⦂○o——

HE that lives ill, fear follows him.

——o○⦂◉⦂○o——

GIVE a clown your finger, and he will take your hand.

——o○⦂◉⦂○o——

GOOD is to be sought out, and evil attended.

——o○⦂◉⦂○o——

A GOOD paymaster starts not at assurances.

——o○⦂◉⦂○o——

No alchemy to saving.

——o○⦂◉⦂○o——

To a grateful man give money when he asks.

——o○⦂◉⦂○o——

WHO would do ill ne'er wants occasion.

——o○⦂◉⦂○o——

To fine folks a little ill finely wrapped.

——o○⦂◉⦂○o——

A child correct behind, and not before.

——o○⦂◉⦂○o——

To a fair day open the window, but make you ready as to a foul one.

——o○⦂◉⦂○o——

KEEP good men company, and you shall be of the number.

———◦◦⦂◎⦂◦◦———

No love to a father's.

———◦◦⦂◎⦂◦◦———

THE mill gets by going.

———◦◦⦂◎⦂◦◦———

To a boiling pot flies come not.

———◦◦⦂◎⦂◦◦———

MAKE haste to an ill way, that you may get out of it.

———◦◦⦂◎⦂◦◦———

A SNOW year, a rich year.

———◦◦⦂◎⦂◦◦———

BETTER to be blind than to see ill.

———◦◦⦂◎⦂◦◦———

LEARN weeping, and thou shalt laugh gaining.

———◦◦⦂◎⦂◦◦———

WHO has no more bread than need must not keep a dog.

———◦◦⦂◎⦂◦◦———

A GARDEN must be looked unto and dressed, as the body.

———◦◦⦂◎⦂◦◦———

THE fox when he cannot reach the grapes, says they are not ripe.

———◦◦⦂◎⦂◦◦———

WATER trotted is as good as oats.

———◦◦⦂◎⦂◦◦———

THOUGH the mastiff be gentle, yet bite him not by the lip.

———◦◦⦂◎⦂◦◦———

THOUGH a lie be well dressed, it is ever overcome.

THOUGH old and wise, yet still advise.

THREE helping one another bear the burden of six.

SLANDER is a shipwreck by a dry tempest.

OLD wine and an old friend are good provisions.

HAPPY is he that chastens himself.

WELL may he smell fire whose gown burns.

THE wrongs of a husband or master are not reproached.

WELCOME evil, if thou comest alone.

LOVE your neighbor, yet pull not down your hedge.

THE bit that one eats, no friend makes.

A DRUNKARD's purse is a bottle.

SHE spins well that breeds her children.

GOOD is the *mora** that makes all sure.

———o○⟨◉⟩○o———

PLAY with a fool at home, and he will play with you in
the market.

———o○⟨◉⟩○o———

EVERY one stretcheth his legs according to his coverlet.

———o○⟨◉⟩○o———

AUTUMNAL agues are long or mortal.

———o○⟨◉⟩○o———

MARRY your son when you will; your daughter when you can.

———o○⟨◉⟩○o———

DALLY not with money or women.

———o○⟨◉⟩○o———

MEN speak of the fair as things went with them there.

———o○⟨◉⟩○o———

THE best remedy against an ill man is much ground
between both.

———o○⟨◉⟩○o———

THE mill cannot grind with the water that's past.

———o○⟨◉⟩○o———

CORN is cleaned with wind, and the soul with chastenings.

———o○⟨◉⟩○o———

GOOD words are worth much, and cost little.

———o○⟨◉⟩○o———

To buy dear is not bounty.

———o○⟨◉⟩○o———

JEST not with the eye, or with religion.

———◦◦ॢ⦿ॢ◦◦———

THE eye and religion can bear no jesting.

———◦◦ॢ⦿ॢ◦◦———

WITHOUT favor none will know you, and with it you will not know yourself.

———◦◦ॢ⦿ॢ◦◦———

BUY at a fair, but sell at home.

———◦◦ॢ⦿ॢ◦◦———

COVER yourself with your shield, and care not for cries.

———◦◦ॢ⦿ॢ◦◦———

A WICKED man's gift has a touch of his master.

———◦◦ॢ⦿ॢ◦◦———

NONE is a fool always, every one sometimes.

———◦◦ॢ⦿ॢ◦◦———

FROM a choleric man withdraw a little, from him that says nothing, for ever.

———◦◦ॢ⦿ॢ◦◦———

DEBTORS are liars.

———◦◦ॢ⦿ॢ◦◦———

OF all smells, bread; of all tastes, salt.

———◦◦ॢ⦿ॢ◦◦———

IN a great river great fish are found; but take heed lest you be drowned.

———◦◦ॢ⦿ॢ◦◦———

EVER since we wear clothes, we know not one another.

———◦◦ॢ⦿ॢ◦◦———

GOD heals, and the physician has the thanks.

————∘∘⟡⊙⟡∘∘————

HELL is full of good meanings and wishings.

————∘∘⟡⊙⟡∘∘————

TAKE heed of still waters, the quick pass away.

————∘∘⟡⊙⟡∘∘————

AFTER the house is finished, leave it.

————∘∘⟡⊙⟡∘∘————

OUR own actions are our security, not others' judgements.

————∘∘⟡⊙⟡∘∘————

THINK of ease, but work on.

————∘∘⟡⊙⟡∘∘————

HE that lies long abed, his estate feels it.

————∘∘⟡⊙⟡∘∘————

WHETHER you boil snow or pound it, you can have but
water of it.

————∘∘⟡⊙⟡∘∘————

ONE stroke fells not an oak.

————∘∘⟡⊙⟡∘∘————

GOD complains not, but does what is fitting.

————∘∘⟡⊙⟡∘∘————

A DILIGENT scholar, and the master's paid.

————∘∘⟡⊙⟡∘∘————

MILK says to wine, "Welcome, friend."

————∘∘⟡⊙⟡∘∘————

THEY that knew one another salute afar off.

———o○≬○o———

WHERE there is no honor there is no grief.

———o○≬○o———

WHERE the drink goes in there the wit goes out.

———o○≬○o———

HE that stays does the business.

———o○≬○o———

ALMS never make poor. Or thus,

———o○≬○o———

GREAT almsgiving lessens no man's living.

———o○≬○o———

GIVING much to the poor does enrich a man's store.

———o○≬○o———

IT takes much from the account, to which his sin doth amount.

———o○≬○o———

IT adds to the glory both of soul and body.

———o○≬○o———

ILL comes in by ells, and goes out by inches.

———o○≬○o———

THE smith and his penny both are black.

———o○≬○o———

WHOSE house is of glass must not throw stones at another.

———o○≬○o———

IF the old dog bark, he gives counsel.

———o○≬○o———

THE tree that grows slowly keeps itself for another.

———∘○ː◎ː○∘———

I WEPT when I was born, and every day shows why.

———∘○ː◎ː○∘———

HE that looks not before finds himself behind.

———∘○ː◎ː○∘———

HE that plays his money ought not to value it.

———∘○ː◎ː○∘———

HE that riseth first is first dressed.

———∘○ː◎ː○∘———

DISEASES of the eye are to be cured with the elbow.

———∘○ː◎ː○∘———

THE hole calls the thief.

———∘○ː◎ː○∘———

A GENTLEMAN's greyhound and a saltbox, seek them at the fire.

———∘○ː◎ː○∘———

A CHILD's service is little, yet he is no little fool that despiseth it.

———∘○ː◎ː○∘———

THE river past, and God forgotten.

———∘○ː◎ː○∘———

EVILS have their comfort; good none can support (to wit) with
a moderate and contented heart.

———∘○ː◎ː○∘———

WHO must account for himself and others must know both.

———∘○ː◎ː○∘———

HE that eats the hard shall eat the ripe.

———✦———

THE miserable man maketh a penny of a farthing, and the liberal of a farthing sixpence.

———✦———

THE honey is sweet, but the bee stings.

———✦———

WEIGHT and measure take away strife.

———✦———

THE son full and tattered, the daughter empty and fine.

———✦———

EVERY path has a puddle.

———✦———

IN good years corn is hay, in ill years straw is corn.

———✦———

SEND a wise man on an errand, and say nothing unto him.

———✦———

IN life you loved me not, in death you bewail me.

———✦———

INTO a mouth shut flies fly not.

———✦———

THE heart's letter is read in the eyes.

———✦———

THE ill that comes out of our mouth falls into our bosom.

———✦———

In great pedigrees there are governors and chandlers.

———○○○○○———

In the house of a fiddler all fiddle.

———○○○○○———

Sometimes the best gain is to lose.

———○○○○○———

Working and making a fire doth discretion require.

———○○○○○———

One grain fills not a sack, but helps his fellows.

———○○○○○———

It is a great victory that comes without blood.

———○○○○○———

In war, hunting, and love, men for one pleasure a thousand griefs prove.

———○○○○○———

Reckon right, and February has one and thirty days.

———○○○○○———

Honor without profit is a ring on the finger.

———○○○○○———

Estate in two parishes is bread in two wallets.

———○○○○○———

Honor and profit lie not in one sack.

———○○○○○———

A naughty child is better sick than whole.

———○○○○○———

TRUTH and oil are ever above.

———◦◦ᦢᦡᦢ◦◦———

HE that riseth betimes* has something in his head.

———◦◦ᦢᦡᦢ◦◦———

ADVISE none to marry or go to war.

———◦◦ᦢᦡᦢ◦◦———

To steal the hog, and give the feet for alms.

———◦◦ᦢᦡᦢ◦◦———

THE thorn comes forth with his point forwards.

———◦◦ᦢᦡᦢ◦◦———

ONE hand washeth another, and both the face.

———◦◦ᦢᦡᦢ◦◦———

THE fault of the horse is put on the saddle.

———◦◦ᦢᦡᦢ◦◦———

THE corn hides itself in the snow as an old man in furs.

———◦◦ᦢᦡᦢ◦◦———

THE Jews spend at Easter, the Moors at marriages, the Christians in suits.

———◦◦ᦢᦡᦢ◦◦———

FINE dressing is a foul house swept before the doors.

———◦◦ᦢᦡᦢ◦◦———

A WOMAN and a glass are ever in danger.

———◦◦ᦢᦡᦢ◦◦———

AN ill wound is cured, not an ill name.

———◦◦ᦢᦡᦢ◦◦———

THE wise hand doth not all that the foolish mouth speaks.

———⚬⚬ᛢ☙⚬⚬———

ON painting and fighting look aloof.

———⚬⚬ᛢ☙⚬⚬———

KNOWLEDGE is folly, except grace guide it.

———⚬⚬ᛢ☙⚬⚬———

PUNISHMENT is lame, but it comes.

———⚬⚬ᛢ☙⚬⚬———

THE more women look in their glass, the less they look to
their house.

———⚬⚬ᛢ☙⚬⚬———

A LONG tongue is a sign of a short hand.

———⚬⚬ᛢ☙⚬⚬———

MARRY a widow before she leave mourning.

———⚬⚬ᛢ☙⚬⚬———

THE worst of law is that one suit breeds twenty.

———⚬⚬ᛢ☙⚬⚬———

PROVIDENCE is better than a rent.

———⚬⚬ᛢ☙⚬⚬———

WHAT your glass tells you will not be told by counsel.

———⚬⚬ᛢ☙⚬⚬———

THERE are more men threatened than stricken.

———⚬⚬ᛢ☙⚬⚬———

A FOOL knows more in his house than a wise man in another's.

———⚬⚬ᛢ☙⚬⚬———

I HAD rather ride on an ass that carries me than a horse that throws me.

———oo⟡⦿⟡oo———

THE hard [man] gives more than he that has nothing.

———oo⟡⦿⟡oo———

THE beast that goes always never wants blows.

———oo⟡⦿⟡oo———

GOOD cheap is dear.

———oo⟡⦿⟡oo———

IT costs more to do ill than to do well.

———oo⟡⦿⟡oo———

GOOD words quench more than a bucket of water.

———oo⟡⦿⟡oo———

AN ill agreement is better than a good judgment.

———oo⟡⦿⟡oo———

THERE is more talk than trouble.

———oo⟡⦿⟡oo———

BETTER spare to have of thine own than ask of other men.

———oo⟡⦿⟡oo———

BETTER good afar off than evil at hand.

———oo⟡⦿⟡oo———

FEAR keeps the garden better than the gardener.

———oo⟡⦿⟡oo———

I HAD rather ask of my sire brown bread than borrow of my neighbor white.

———oo⟡⦿⟡oo———

YOUR pot broken seems better than my whole one.

———οο᷈ᴏⳠᴏⳠοο———

LET an ill man lie in thy straw and he looks to be thy heir.

———οο᷈ᴏⳠᴏⳠοο———

BY suppers more have been killed than Galen ever cured.

———οο᷈ᴏⳠᴏⳠοο———

WHILE the discreet advise, the fool does his business.

———οο᷈ᴏⳠᴏⳠοο———

A MOUNTAIN and a river are good neighbors.

———οο᷈ᴏⳠᴏⳠοο———

GOSSIPS are frogs, they drink and talk.

———οο᷈ᴏⳠᴏⳠοο———

MUCH spends the traveller more than the abider.

———οο᷈ᴏⳠᴏⳠοο———

PRAYERS and provender hinder no journey.

———οο᷈ᴏⳠᴏⳠοο———

A WELL bred youth neither speaks of himself, nor being
spoken to, is silent.

———οο᷈ᴏⳠᴏⳠοο———

A JOURNEYING women speaks much of all, and all of her.

———οο᷈ᴏⳠᴏⳠοο———

THE fox knows much, but more he that catcheth him.

———οο᷈ᴏⳠᴏⳠοο———

MANY friends in general, one in special.

———οο᷈ᴏⳠᴏⳠοο———

THE fool asks much, but he is more fool that grants it.

———⋅∘⦂⊕⦂∘⋅———

MANY kiss the hand they wish cut off.

———⋅∘⦂⊕⦂∘⋅———

NEITHER bribe, nor lose thy right.

———⋅∘⦂⊕⦂∘⋅———

IN the world who knows not to swim goes to the bottom.

———⋅∘⦂⊕⦂∘⋅———

CHOOSE not a house near an inn (*viz.* for noise), or in a
corner (for filth).

———⋅∘⦂⊕⦂∘⋅———

HE is a fool that thinks not that another thinks.

———⋅∘⦂⊕⦂∘⋅———

NEITHER eyes on letters, nor hands in coffers.

———⋅∘⦂⊕⦂∘⋅———

THE lion is not so fierce as they paint him.

———⋅∘⦂⊕⦂∘⋅———

Go not for every grief to the physician, nor for every quarrel
to the lawyer, nor for every thirst to the pot.

———⋅∘⦂⊕⦂∘⋅———

GOOD service is a great enchantment.

———⋅∘⦂⊕⦂∘⋅———

THERE would be no great ones if there were no little ones.

———⋅∘⦂⊕⦂∘⋅———

IT is no sure rule to fish with a cross-bow.

———⋅∘⦂⊕⦂∘⋅———

THERE were no ill language if it were not ill taken.

———◦◦ː◦ː◦◦———

THE groundsel* speaks not, save what it heard at the hinges.

———◦◦ː◦ː◦◦———

THE best mirror is an old friend.

———◦◦ː◦ː◦◦———

SAY no ill of the year till it be past.

———◦◦ː◦ː◦◦———

A MAN's discontent is his worst evil.

———◦◦ː◦ː◦◦———

FEAR nothing but sin.

———◦◦ː◦ː◦◦———

THE child says nothing but what it heard by the fire.

———◦◦ː◦ː◦◦———

CALL me not an olive till thou see me gathered.

———◦◦ː◦ː◦◦———

THAT is not good language which all understand not.

———◦◦ː◦ː◦◦———

HE that burns his house warms himself for once.

———◦◦ː◦ː◦◦———

HE will burn his house to warm his hands.

———◦◦ː◦ː◦◦———

HE will spend a whole year's rent at one meal's meat.

———◦◦ː◦ː◦◦———

ALL is not gold that glitters.

———◦◦ː◦ː◦◦———

A BLUSTERING night, a fair day.

BE not idle, and you shall not be longing.

HE is not poor that has little, but he that desireth much.

LET none say, I will not drink water.

HE wrongs not an old man that steals his supper from him.

THE tongue talks at the head's cost.

HE that strikes with his tongue must ward* with his head.

KEEP not ill men company, lest you increase the number.

GOD strikes not with both hands, for to the sea He made heavens, and to rivers fords.

A RUGGED stone grows smooth from hand to hand.

NO lock will hold against the power of gold.

THE absent party is still faulty.

PEACE and patience, and death with repentance.

———oo⟡oo———

IF you lose your time, you cannot get money nor gain.

———oo⟡oo———

BE not a baker if your head be of butter.

———oo⟡oo———

ASK much to have a little.

———oo⟡oo———

LITTLE sticks kindle the fire; great ones put it out.

———oo⟡oo———

ANOTHER's bread costs dear.

———oo⟡oo———

ALTHOUGH it rain, throw not away thy watering-pot.

———oo⟡oo———

ALTHOUGH the sun shine, leave not thy cloak at home.

———oo⟡oo———

A LITTLE with quiet is the only diet.

———oo⟡oo———

IN vain is the mill-clack,* if the miller his hearing lack.

———oo⟡oo———

BY the needle you shall draw the thread, and by that which is past see how that which is to come will be drawn on.

———oo⟡oo———

STAY a little, and news will find you.

———oo⟡oo———

STAY till the lame messenger come, if you will know the truth of the thing.

——◦◦⊱◉⊰◦◦——

WHEN God will, no wind but brings rain.

——◦◦⊱◉⊰◦◦——

THOUGH you rise early, yet the day comes at his time and not till then.

——◦◦⊱◉⊰◦◦——

PULL down your hat on the wind's side.

——◦◦⊱◉⊰◦◦——

As the year is, your pot must seethe.

——◦◦⊱◉⊰◦◦——

SINCE you know all, and I nothing, tell me what I dreamed last night.

——◦◦⊱◉⊰◦◦——

WHEN the fox preacheth, beware geese.

——◦◦⊱◉⊰◦◦——

WHEN you are an anvil, hold you still; when you are a hammer, strike your fill.

——◦◦⊱◉⊰◦◦——

POOR and liberal, rich and covetous.

——◦◦⊱◉⊰◦◦——

HE that makes his bed ill, lies there.

——◦◦⊱◉⊰◦◦——

HE that labors and thrives, spins gold.

——◦◦⊱◉⊰◦◦——

He that sows, trusts in God.

———∘∘⋅⊙⋅∘∘———

He that lies with the dogs, riseth with fleas.

———∘∘⋅⊙⋅∘∘———

He that repairs not a part, builds all.

———∘∘⋅⊙⋅∘∘———

A discontented man knows not where to sit easy.

———∘∘⋅⊙⋅∘∘———

Who spits against heaven, it falls in his face.

———∘∘⋅⊙⋅∘∘———

He that dines and leaves, lays the cloth twice.

———∘∘⋅⊙⋅∘∘———

Who eats his cock alone, must saddle his horse alone.

———∘∘⋅⊙⋅∘∘———

He that is not handsome at twenty, nor strong at thirty, nor rich at forty, nor wise at fifty, will never be handsome, strong, rich, or wise.

———∘∘⋅⊙⋅∘∘———

He that does what he will, does not what he ought.

———∘∘⋅⊙⋅∘∘———

He that will deceive the fox must rise betimes.*

———∘∘⋅⊙⋅∘∘———

He that lives well sees afar off.

———∘∘⋅⊙⋅∘∘———

He that has a mouth of his own, must not say to another, Blow.

———∘∘⋅⊙⋅∘∘———

HE that will be served must be patient.

———o₀ː◎ː₀o———

HE that gives thee a bone would not have thee die.

———o₀ː◎ː₀o———

HE that chastens one chastens twenty.

———o₀ː◎ː₀o———

HE that has lost his credit is dead to the world.

———o₀ː◎ː₀o———

HE that has no ill fortune is troubled with good.

———o₀ː◎ː₀o———

HE that demands, misseth not, unless his demands be foolish.

———o₀ː◎ː₀o———

HE that has no honey in his pot, let him have it in his mouth.

———o₀ː◎ː₀o———

HE that takes not up a pin, slights his wife.

———o₀ː◎ː₀o———

HE that owes nothing, if he makes not mouths at us,
is courteous.

———o₀ː◎ː₀o———

HE that loseth his due gets not thanks.

———o₀ː◎ː₀o———

HE that believes all, misseth; he that believeth nothing, hits not.

———o₀ː◎ː₀o———

PARDONS and pleasantness are great revenges of slander.

———o₀ː◎ː₀o———

A MARRIED man turns his staff into a stake.

IF you would know secrets, look for them in grief or pleasure.

SERVE a noble disposition, though poor, the time comes that he will repay thee.

THE fault is as great as he that is faulty.

IF folly were grief, every house would weep.

HE that would be well old must be old betimes.*

SIT in your place, and none can make you rise.

IF you could run as you drink you might catch a hare.

WOULD you know what money is, go borrow some.

THE morning sun never lasts a day.

THOU hast death in thy house and dost bewail another's.

WHATEVER is made by the hand of man, by the hand of man may be overturned.

ALL griefs with bread are less.

———∘○⦂◉⦂○∘———

ALL things require skill but an appetite.

———∘○⦂◉⦂○∘———

ALL things have their place, knew we how to place them.

———∘○⦂◉⦂○∘———

LITTLE pitchers have wide ears.

———∘○⦂◉⦂○∘———

WE are fools one to another.

———∘○⦂◉⦂○∘———

THIS world is nothing except it tend to another.

———∘○⦂◉⦂○∘———

THERE are three ways—the universities, the sea, the court.

———∘○⦂◉⦂○∘———

GOD comes to see without a bell.

———∘○⦂◉⦂○∘———

LIFE without a friend is death without a witness.

———∘○⦂◉⦂○∘———

CLOTHE thee in war, arm thee in peace.

———∘○⦂◉⦂○∘———

THE horse thinks one thing, and he that saddles him another.

———∘○⦂◉⦂○∘———

MILLS and wives ever want.

———∘○⦂◉⦂○∘———

THE dog that licks ashes trust not with meal.

———∘○⦂◉⦂○∘———

THE buyer needs a hundred eyes, the seller not one.

———o⚬⚬⚬⚬———

HE carries well to whom it weighs not.

———o⚬⚬⚬⚬———

THE comforter's head never aches.

———o⚬⚬⚬⚬———

STEP after step the ladder is ascended.

———o⚬⚬⚬⚬———

WHO likes not the drink, God deprives him of bread.

———o⚬⚬⚬⚬———

To a crazy ship all winds are contrary.

———o⚬⚬⚬⚬———

JUSTICE pleaseth few in their own house.

———o⚬⚬⚬⚬———

IN time comes he whom God sends.

———o⚬⚬⚬⚬———

WATER afar off quencheth not fire.

———o⚬⚬⚬⚬———

IN sports and journeys men are known.

———o⚬⚬⚬⚬———

AN old friend is a new house.

———o⚬⚬⚬⚬———

LOVE is not found in the market.

———o⚬⚬⚬⚬———

DRY feet, warm head, bring safe to bed.

———o⚬⚬⚬⚬———

HE is rich enough that wants nothing.

———o○;◎;○o———

ONE father is enough to govern one hundred sons, but not a hundred sons one father.

———o○;◎;○o———

FAR shooting never killed bird.

———o○;◎;○o———

AN upbraided morsel never choked any.

———o○;◎;○o———

DEARTHS foreseen come not.

———o○;◎;○o———

AN ill laborer quarrels with his tools.

———o○;◎;○o———

HE that falls into the dirt, the longer he stays there the fouler he is.

———o○;◎;○o———

HE that blames would buy.

———o○;◎;○o———

HE that sings on Friday will weep on Sunday.

———o○;◎;○o———

THE charges of building and making of gardens are unknown.

———o○;◎;○o———

MY house, my house, though thou art small, thou art to me the Escurial.*

———o○;◎;○o———

A HUNDRED load of thought will not pay one of debts.

———o○;◎;○o———

HE that comes of a hen must scrape.

———oo⟡oo———

HE that seeks trouble never misses.

———oo⟡oo———

HE that once deceives is ever suspected.

———oo⟡oo———

BEING on sea, sail; being on land, settle.

———oo⟡oo———

WHO does his own business fouls not his hands.

———oo⟡oo———

HE that makes a good war makes a good peace.

———oo⟡oo———

HE that works after his own manner his head aches not at
the matter.

———oo⟡oo———

WHO has bitter in his mouth spits not all sweet.

———oo⟡oo———

HE that has children, all his morsels are not his own.

———oo⟡oo———

HE that has the spices may season as he list.

———oo⟡oo———

HE that has a head of wax must not walk in the sun.

———oo⟡oo———

HE that has love in his breast has spurs in his side.

———oo⟡oo———

HE that respects not is not respected.

———◦○⅋◎⅋○◦———

HE that has a fox for his mate has need of a net at his girdle.

———◦○⅋◎⅋○◦———

HE that has right, fears; he that has wrong, hopes.

———◦○⅋◎⅋○◦———

HE that has patience, has fat thrushes for a farthing.

———◦○⅋◎⅋○◦———

NEVER was strumpet* fair.

———◦○⅋◎⅋○◦———

HE that measures not himself is measured.

———◦○⅋◎⅋○◦———

HE that has one hog makes him fat; and he that has one son makes him a fool.

———◦○⅋◎⅋○◦———

WHO lets his wife go to every feast, and his horse drink at every water, shall neither have good wife nor good horse.

———◦○⅋◎⅋○◦———

HE that speaks sows, and he that holds his peace gathers.

———◦○⅋◎⅋○◦———

HE that has little is the less dirty.

———◦○⅋◎⅋○◦———

HE that lives most dies most.

———◦○⅋◎⅋○◦———

HE that has one foot in the straw has another in the spital.*

———◦○⅋◎⅋○◦———

HE that is fed at another's hand may stay long ere he be full.

———◦◦⟡◦◦———

HE that makes a thing too fine breaks it.

———◦◦⟡◦◦———

HE that bewails himself has the cure in his hands.

———◦◦⟡◦◦———

HE that would be well needs not go from his own house.

———◦◦⟡◦◦———

COUNSEL breaks not the head.

———◦◦⟡◦◦———

FLY the pleasure that bites tomorrow.

———◦◦⟡◦◦———

HE that knows what may be gained in a day never steals.

———◦◦⟡◦◦———

MONEY refused loseth its brightness.

———◦◦⟡◦◦———

HEALTH and money go far.

———◦◦⟡◦◦———

WHERE your will is ready your feet are light.

———◦◦⟡◦◦———

A great ship asks deep waters.

———◦◦⟡◦◦———

WOE to the house where there is no chiding.

———◦◦⟡◦◦———

TAKE heed of the vinegar of sweet wine.

———◦◦⟡◦◦———

FOOLS bite one another, but wise men agree together.

———◦◦ᢀᢀ◦◦———

TRUST not one night's ice.

———◦◦ᢀᢀ◦◦———

GOOD is good, but better carries it.

———◦◦ᢀᢀ◦◦———

To gain teacheth how to spend.

———◦◦ᢀᢀ◦◦———

GOOD finds good.

———◦◦ᢀᢀ◦◦———

THE dog gnaws the bone because he cannot swallow it.

———◦◦ᢀᢀ◦◦———

THE crow bewails the sheep, and then eats it.

———◦◦ᢀᢀ◦◦———

BUILDING is a sweet impoverishing.

———◦◦ᢀᢀ◦◦———

THE first degree of folly is to hold one's self wise, the second to profess it, the third to despise counsel.

———◦◦ᢀᢀ◦◦———

THE greatest step is that out of doors.

———◦◦ᢀᢀ◦◦———

To weep for joy is a kind of manna.

———◦◦ᢀᢀ◦◦———

THE first service a child doeth his father is to make him foolish.

———◦◦ᢀᢀ◦◦———

THE resolved mind has no cares.

———◦○❀○◦———

IN the kingdom of a cheater the wallet is carried before.

———◦○❀○◦———

THE eye will have his part.

———◦○❀○◦———

THE good mother says not, "Will you?" but gives.

———◦○❀○◦———

A HOUSE and a woman suit excellently.

———◦○❀○◦———

IN the kingdom of blind men the one-eyed is king.

———◦○❀○◦———

A LITTLE kitchen makes a large house.

———◦○❀○◦———

WAR makes thieves, and peace hangs them.

———◦○❀○◦———

POVERTY is the mother of health.

———◦○❀○◦———

IN the morning mountains, in the evening fountains.

———◦○❀○◦———

THE back door robs the house.

———◦○❀○◦———

WEALTH is like rheum,* it falls on the weakest parts.

———◦○❀○◦———

THE gown is his that wears it, and the world his that enjoys it.

———◦○❀○◦———

HOPE is the poor man's bread.

———◦◦⦂⦂◦◦———

VIRTUE now is in herbs, and stones, and words only.

———◦◦⦂⦂◦◦———

FINE words dress ill deeds.

———◦◦⦂⦂◦◦———

LABOR is long lived, pray as even dying.

———◦◦⦂⦂◦◦———

A POOR beauty finds more lovers than husbands.

———◦◦⦂⦂◦◦———

DISCREET women have neither eyes nor ears.

———◦◦⦂⦂◦◦———

THINGS well fitted abide.

———◦◦⦂⦂◦◦———

PRETTINESS dies first.

———◦◦⦂⦂◦◦———

TALKING pays no toll.

———◦◦⦂⦂◦◦———

THE master's eye fattens the horse, and his foot the ground.

———◦◦⦂⦂◦◦———

DISGRACES are like cherries, one draws another.

———◦◦⦂⦂◦◦———

PRAISE a hill, but keep below.

———◦◦⦂⦂◦◦———

PRAISE the sea, but keep on land.

———◦◦⦂⦂◦◦———

IN choosing a wife, and buying a sword, we ought not to trust another.

———◦◦⟡◦◦———

THE wearer knows where the shoe wrings.

———◦◦⟡◦◦———

FAIR is not fair, but that which pleaseth.

———◦◦⟡◦◦———

THERE is no jollity but has a smack of folly.

———◦◦⟡◦◦———

HE that's long a-giving knows not how to give.

———◦◦⟡◦◦———

THE filth under the white snow the sun discovers.

———◦◦⟡◦◦———

EVERY one fastens where there is gain.

———◦◦⟡◦◦———

ALL feet tread not in one shoe.

———◦◦⟡◦◦———

PATIENCE, time, and money accommodate all things.

———◦◦⟡◦◦———

FOR want of a nail the shoe is lost, for want of a shoe the horse is lost, for want of a horse the rider is lost.

———◦◦⟡◦◦———

WEIGH justly, and sell dearly.

———◦◦⟡◦◦———

LITTLE wealth, little care.

———◦◦⟡◦◦———

LITTLE journeys and good cost bring safe home.

———∘₀⁚☙⁚₀∘———

GLUTTONY kills more than the sword.

———∘₀⁚☙⁚₀∘———

WHEN children stand quiet they have done some ill.

———∘₀⁚☙⁚₀∘———

A LITTLE and good fills the trencher.*

———∘₀⁚☙⁚₀∘———

A PENNY spared is twice got.

———∘₀⁚☙⁚₀∘———

WHEN a knave* is in a plum-tree he has neither friend nor kin.

———∘₀⁚☙⁚₀∘———

SHORT boughs, long vintage.

———∘₀⁚☙⁚₀∘———

HEALTH without money is half an ague.*

———∘₀⁚☙⁚₀∘———

IF the wise erred not it would go hard with fools.

———∘₀⁚☙⁚₀∘———

BEAR with evil and expect good.

———∘₀⁚☙⁚₀∘———

HE that tells a secret is another's servant.

———∘₀⁚☙⁚₀∘———

IF all fools wore white caps we should seem a flock of geese.

———∘₀⁚☙⁚₀∘———

WATER, fire and soldiers quickly make room.

———∘₀⁚☙⁚₀∘———

PENSION never enriched a young man.

———◦○⤆⚬⤇○◦———

UNDER water, famine; under snow, bread.

———◦○⤆⚬⤇○◦———

THE lame goes as far as your staggerer.

———◦○⤆⚬⤇○◦———

HE that loseth is a merchant as well as he that gains.

———◦○⤆⚬⤇○◦———

A JADE eats as much as a good horse.

———◦○⤆⚬⤇○◦———

ALL things in their being are good for something.

———◦○⤆⚬⤇○◦———

ONE flower makes no garland.

———◦○⤆⚬⤇○◦———

A FAIR death honors the whole life.

———◦○⤆⚬⤇○◦———

ONE enemy is too much.

———◦○⤆⚬⤇○◦———

LIVING well is the best revenge.

———◦○⤆⚬⤇○◦———

ONE fool makes a hundred.

———◦○⤆⚬⤇○◦———

ONE pair of ears draws dry a hundred tongues.

———◦○⤆⚬⤇○◦———

YOUR thoughts close and your countenance loose.

———◦○⤆⚬⤇○◦———

A FOOL may throw a stone into a well, which a hundred wise
men cannot pull out.

———∘∘⚬⊙⚬∘∘———

ONE slumber finds another.

———∘∘⚬⊙⚬∘∘———

ON a good bargain think twice.

———∘∘⚬⊙⚬∘∘———

To a good spender God is the treasurer.

———∘∘⚬⊙⚬∘∘———

A CURST cow has short horns.

———∘∘⚬⊙⚬∘∘———

MUSIC helps not the toothache.

———∘∘⚬⊙⚬∘∘———

WE cannot come to honor under coverlet.

———∘∘⚬⊙⚬∘∘———

GREAT pains quickly find ease.

———∘∘⚬⊙⚬∘∘———

To the counsel of fools a wooden bell.

———∘∘⚬⊙⚬∘∘———

THE choleric man never wants woe.

———∘∘⚬⊙⚬∘∘———

HELP thyself, and God will help thee.

———∘∘⚬⊙⚬∘∘———

AT the game's end we shall see who gains.

———∘∘⚬⊙⚬∘∘———

THERE are many ways to fame.

———∘∘⚬⚬∘∘———

LOVE is the true price of love.

———∘∘⚬⚬∘∘———

LOVE rules his kingdom without a sword.

———∘∘⚬⚬∘∘———

LOVE makes all hard hearts gentle.

———∘∘⚬⚬∘∘———

LOVE makes a good eye squint.

———∘∘⚬⚬∘∘———

LOVE asks faith, and faith firmness.

———∘∘⚬⚬∘∘———

A SCEPTER is one thing, and a ladle another.

———∘∘⚬⚬∘∘———

GREAT trees are good for nothing but shade.

———∘∘⚬⚬∘∘———

HE commands enough that obeys a wise man.

———∘∘⚬⚬∘∘———

FAIR words make me look to my purse.

———∘∘⚬⚬∘∘———

THOUGH the fox run, the chicken has wings.

———∘∘⚬⚬∘∘———

HE plays well that wins.

———∘∘⚬⚬∘∘———

MONEY wants no followers.

———∘∘⚬⚬∘∘———

You must strike in measure when there are many to strike on one anvil.

———oo∘○∘oo———

The shortest answer is doing.

———oo∘○∘oo———

It is a poor stake that cannot stand one year in the ground.

———oo∘○∘oo———

He that commits a fault thinks everyone speaks of it.

———oo∘○∘oo———

He that is foolish in the fault, let him be wise in the punishment.

———oo∘○∘oo———

The blind eats many a fly.

———oo∘○∘oo———

He that can make a fire well can end a quarrel.

———oo∘○∘oo———

The toothache is more ease than to deal with ill people.

———oo∘○∘oo———

He that would have what he has not should do what he does not.

———oo∘○∘oo———

He that has no good trade, it is to his loss.

———oo∘○∘oo———

The offender never pardons.

———oo∘○∘oo———

He that lives not well one year sorrows seven after.

———oo∘○∘oo———

HE that hopes not for good fears not evil.

———oༀ☼ༀoo———

HE that is angry at a feast is rude.

———oༀ☼ༀoo———

HE that mocks a cripple ought to be whole.

———oༀ☼ༀoo———

WHEN the tree is fallen all go with their hatchet.

———oༀ☼ༀoo———

HE that has horns in his bosom let him not put them on
his head.

———oༀ☼ༀoo———

HE that burns most shines most.

———oༀ☼ༀoo———

HE that trusts in a lie shall perish in truth.

———oༀ☼ༀoo———

HE that blows in the dust fills his eyes with it.

———oༀ☼ༀoo———

BELLS call others, but themselves enter not into the church.

———oༀ☼ༀoo———

OF fair things the autumn is fair.

———oༀ☼ༀoo———

GIVING is dead, restoring very sick.

———oༀ☼ༀoo———

A GIFT much expected is paid, not given.

———oༀ☼ༀoo———

Two ill meals make the third a glutton.

——⊶⊙⊷——

THE royal crown cures not the headache.

——⊶⊙⊷——

'TIS hard to be wretched, but worse to be known so.

——⊶⊙⊷——

A FEATHER in hand is better than a bird in the air.

——⊶⊙⊷——

IT is better to be the head of a lizard than the tail of a lion.

——⊶⊙⊷——

GOOD and quickly seldom meet.

——⊶⊙⊷——

FOLLY grows without watering.

——⊶⊙⊷——

HAPPIER are the hands compassed with iron, than a heart
with thoughts.

——⊶⊙⊷——

IF the staff be crooked, the shadow cannot be straight.

——⊶⊙⊷——

To take the nuts from the fire with the dog's foot.

——⊶⊙⊷——

HE is a fool that makes a wedge of his fist.

——⊶⊙⊷——

VALOR that parleys is near yielding.

——⊶⊙⊷——

THURSDAY come and the week is gone.

———

A FLATTERER's throat is an open sepulchre.

———

THERE is great force hidden in a sweet command.

———

THE command of custom is great.

———

To have money is a fear, not to have it a grief.

———

THE cat sees not the mouse ever.

———

LITTLE dogs start the hare, the great get her.

———

WILLOWS are weak, yet they bind other wood.

———

A GOOD payer is master of another's purse.

———

THE thread breaks where it is weakest.

———

OLD men, when they scorn young, make much of death.

———

GOD is at the end, when we think he is furthest off it.

———

A GOOD judge conceives quickly, judges slowly.

———

Rivers need a spring.

———⊸⊶———

He that contemplates has a day without night.

———⊸⊶———

Give losers leave to talk.

———⊸⊶———

Loss embraceth shame.

———⊸⊶———

Gaming, women, and wine, while they laugh, they make men pine.

———⊸⊶———

The fat man knoweth not what the lean thinketh.

———⊸⊶———

Wood half burnt is easily kindled.

———⊸⊶———

The fish adores the bait.

———⊸⊶———

He that goes far has many encounters.

———⊸⊶———

Every bee's honey is sweet.

———⊸⊶———

The slothful is the servant of the counters.

———⊸⊶———

Wisdom has one foot on land and another on the sea.

———⊸⊶———

THE thought has good legs, and the quill a good tongue.

———∞o✧⊙✧o∞———

A WISE man needs not blush for changing his purpose.

———∞o✧⊙✧o∞———

THE March sun raises, but dissolves not.

———∞o✧⊙✧o∞———

TIME is the rider that breaks youth.

———∞o✧⊙✧o∞———

THE wine in the bottle does not quench thirst.

———∞o✧⊙✧o∞———

THE sight of a man has the force of a lion.

———∞o✧⊙✧o∞———

AN examined enterprise goes on boldly.

———∞o✧⊙✧o∞———

IN every art it is good to have a master.

———∞o✧⊙✧o∞———

IN every country dogs bite.

———∞o✧⊙✧o∞———

IN every country the sun rises in the morning.

———∞o✧⊙✧o∞———

A NOBLE plant suits not with a stubborn ground.

———∞o✧⊙✧o∞———

YOU may bring a horse to the river, but he will drink when
and what he pleaseth.

———∞o✧⊙✧o∞———

BEFORE you make a friend, eat a bushel of salt with him.

————o○⦂◎⦂○o————

SPEAK fitly, or be silent wisely.

————o○⦂◎⦂○o————

SKILL and confidence are an unconquered army.

————o○⦂◎⦂○o————

I WAS taken by a morsel, says the fish.

————o○⦂◎⦂○o————

A DISARMED peace is weak.

————o○⦂◎⦂○o————

THE balance distinguisheth not between gold and lead.

————o○⦂◎⦂○o————

THE persuasion of the fortunate sways the doubtful.

————o○⦂◎⦂○o————

To be beloved is above all bargains.

————o○⦂◎⦂○o————

To deceive oneself is very easy.

————o○⦂◎⦂○o————

THE reasons of the poor weigh not.

————o○⦂◎⦂○o————

PERVERSENESS makes one squint-eyed.

————o○⦂◎⦂○o————

THE evening praises the day, and the morning a frost.

————o○⦂◎⦂○o————

THE table robs more than a thief.

————o○⦂◎⦂○o————

WHEN age is jocund it makes sport for death.

———∘∘⦂⊚⦂∘∘———

TRUE praise roots and spreads.

———∘∘⦂⊚⦂∘∘———

FEARS are divided in the midst.

———∘∘⦂⊚⦂∘∘———

THE soul needs few things, the body many.

———∘∘⦂⊚⦂∘∘———

ASTROLOGY is true but the astrologers cannot find it.

———∘∘⦂⊚⦂∘∘———

TIE it well, and let it go.

———∘∘⦂⊚⦂∘∘———

EMPTY vessels sound most.

———∘∘⦂⊚⦂∘∘———

SEND not a cat for lard.

———∘∘⦂⊚⦂∘∘———

FOOLISH tongues talk by the dozen.

———∘∘⦂⊚⦂∘∘———

LOVE makes one fit for any work.

———∘∘⦂⊚⦂∘∘———

A PITIFUL mother makes a scald head.

———∘∘⦂⊚⦂∘∘———

AN old physician, and a young lawyer.

———∘∘⦂⊚⦂∘∘———

TALK much and err much, says the Spaniard.

———∘∘⦂⊚⦂∘∘———

SOME make a conscience of spitting in the church, yet rob the altar.

———o○¿◎¿○o———

AN idle head is a box for the wind.

———o○¿◎¿○o———

SHOW me a liar and I will show thee a thief.

———o○¿◎¿○o———

A BEAN in liberty is better than a comfit* in prison.

———o○¿◎¿○o———

NONE is born master.

———o○¿◎¿○o———

SHOW a good man his error, and he turns it to a virtue; but an ill, it doubles his fault.

———o○¿◎¿○o———

NONE is offended but by himself.

———o○¿◎¿○o———

NONE says his garner is full.

———o○¿◎¿○o———

IN the husband wisdom, in the wife gentleness.

———o○¿◎¿○o———

NOTHING dries sooner than a tear.

———o○¿◎¿○o———

IN a leopard the spots are not observed.

———o○¿◎¿○o———

NOTHING lasts but the Church.

———o○¿◎¿○o———

A WISE man cares not for what he cannot have.

———∘∘ఘ⊚ఘ∘∘———

IT is not good fishing before the net.

———∘∘ఘ⊚ఘ∘∘———

HE cannot be virtuous that is not rigorous.

———∘∘ఘ⊚ఘ∘∘———

THAT which will not be spun, let it not come between the spindle and the distaff.

———∘∘ఘ⊚ఘ∘∘———

WHEN my house burns it is not good playing at chess.

———∘∘ఘ⊚ఘ∘∘———

No barber shaves so close but another finds work.

———∘∘ఘ⊚ఘ∘∘———

THERE is no great banquet, but some fares ill.

———∘∘ఘ⊚ఘ∘∘———

A HOLY habit cleanseth not a foul soul.

———∘∘ఘ⊚ఘ∘∘———

FORBEAR not sowing because of birds.

———∘∘ఘ⊚ఘ∘∘———

MENTION not a halter* in the house of him that was hanged.

———∘∘ఘ⊚ఘ∘∘———

SPEAK not of a dead man at the table.

———∘∘ఘ⊚ఘ∘∘———

A HAT is not made for one shower.

———∘∘ఘ⊚ఘ∘∘———

No sooner is a temple built to God but the devil builds a chapel hard by.

———

Every one puts his fault on the times.

———

You cannot make a windmill go with a pair of bellows.

———

Pardon all but thyself.

———

Every one is weary, the poor in seeking, the rich in keeping, the good in learning.

———

The escaped mouse ever feels the taste of the bait.

———

A little wind kindles, much puts out the fire.

———

Dry bread at home is better than roast meat abroad.

———

More have repented speech than silence.

———

The covetous spends more than the liberal.

———

Divine ashes are better than earthly meal.

———

Beauty draws more than oxen.

———

ONE father is more than a hundred schoolmasters.

————∘∘⟊⊙⟊∘∘————

ONE eye of the master's sees more than ten of the servant's.

————∘∘⟊⊙⟊∘∘————

WHEN God will punish, He will first take away
the understanding.

————∘∘⟊⊙⟊∘∘————

A little labor, much health.

————∘∘⟊⊙⟊∘∘————

WHEN it thunders the thief becomes honest.

————∘∘⟊⊙⟊∘∘————

THE tree that God plants no wind hurts it.

————∘∘⟊⊙⟊∘∘————

KNOWLEDGE is no burden.

————∘∘⟊⊙⟊∘∘————

IT is a bold mouse that nestles in the cat's ear.

————∘∘⟊⊙⟊∘∘————

LONG jesting was never good.

————∘∘⟊⊙⟊∘∘————

IF a good man thrive, all thrive with him.

————∘∘⟊⊙⟊∘∘————

IF the mother had not been in the oven, she had never sought
her daughter there.

————∘∘⟊⊙⟊∘∘————

IF great men would have care of little ones, both would last long.

————∘∘⟊⊙⟊∘∘————

THOUGH you see a churchman ill, yet continue in the church still.

———∘∘⟡∘∘———

OLD praise dies, unless you feed it.

———∘∘⟡∘∘———

IF things were to be done twice, all would be wise.

———∘∘⟡∘∘———

HAD you the world on your chess-board, you could not fill all to your mind.

———∘∘⟡∘∘———

SUFFER and expect.

———∘∘⟡∘∘———

IF fools should not fool it they should lose their season.

———∘∘⟡∘∘———

LOVE and business teach eloquence.

———∘∘⟡∘∘———

THAT which two will takes effect.

———∘∘⟡∘∘———

HE complains wrongfully of the sea, that twice suffers shipwreck.

———∘∘⟡∘∘———

HE is only bright that shines by himself.

———∘∘⟡∘∘———

A VALIANT man's look is more than a coward's sword.

———∘∘⟡∘∘———

THE effect speaks, the tongue needs not.

———∘∘⟡∘∘———

DIVINE grace was never slow.

———∘◦⦂◉⦂◦∘———

REASON lies between the spur and the bridle.

———∘◦⦂◉⦂◦∘———

IT is a proud horse that will not carry his own provender.

———∘◦⦂◉⦂◦∘———

THREE women make a market.

———∘◦⦂◉⦂◦∘———

THREE can hold their peace if two be away.

———∘◦⦂◉⦂◦∘———

IT is an ill counsel that has no escape.

———∘◦⦂◉⦂◦∘———

ALL our pomp the earth covers.

———∘◦⦂◉⦂◦∘———

To whirl the eyes too much shows a kite's brain.

———∘◦⦂◉⦂◦∘———

COMPARISONS are odious.

———∘◦⦂◉⦂◦∘———

ALL keys hang not on one girdle.

———∘◦⦂◉⦂◦∘———

GREAT businesses turn on a little pin.

———∘◦⦂◉⦂◦∘———

THE wind in one's face makes one wise.

———∘◦⦂◉⦂◦∘———

ALL the arms of England will not arm fear.

———∘◦⦂◉⦂◦∘———

ONE sword keeps another in the sheath.

——•◦○◦○◦○◦○•——

BE what thou wouldst seem to be.

——•◦○◦○◦○◦○•——

LET all live as they would die.

——•◦○◦○◦○◦○•——

A gentle heart is tied with an easy thread.

——•◦○◦○◦○◦○•——

SWEET discourse makes short days and nights.

——•◦○◦○◦○◦○•——

GOD provides for him that trusteth.

——•◦○◦○◦○◦○•——

HE that will not have peace, God gives him war.

——•◦○◦○◦○◦○•——

To him that will, ways are not wanting.

——•◦○◦○◦○◦○•——

To a great night a great lanthorn.*

——•◦○◦○◦○◦○•——

To a child all weather is cold.

——•◦○◦○◦○◦○•——

WHERE there is peace God is.

——•◦○◦○◦○◦○•——

NONE is so wise but the fool overtakes him.

——•◦○◦○◦○◦○•——

FOOLS give to please all but their own.

——•◦○◦○◦○◦○•——

PROSPERITY lets go the bridle.

———o⚬∶❀∶⚬o———

THE friar preached against stealing, and had a goose in his sleeve.

———o⚬∶❀∶⚬o———

To be too busy gets contempt.

———o⚬∶❀∶⚬o———

FEBRUARY makes a bridge, and March breaks it.

———o⚬∶❀∶⚬o———

A horse stumbles that has four legs.

———o⚬∶❀∶⚬o———

THE best smell is bread, the best savor salt, the best love that of children.

———o⚬∶❀∶⚬o———

THAT is the best gown that goes up and down the house.

———o⚬∶❀∶⚬o———

THE market is the best garden.

———o⚬∶❀∶⚬o———

A MAN's destiny is always dark.

———o⚬∶❀∶⚬o———

EVERY man's censure is first molded in his own nature.

———o⚬∶❀∶⚬o———

THE virtue of a coward is suspicion.

———o⚬∶❀∶⚬o———

SOLDIERS in peace are like chimneys in summer.

———o⚬∶❀∶⚬o———

THE first dish pleaseth all.

———

THE higher the ape goes the more he shows his tail.

———

NIGHT is the mother of counsel.

———

GOD's mill grinds slow, but sure.

———

EVERY one thinks his sack heaviest.

———

DROUGHT never brought dearth.

———

ALL complain.

———

GAMESTERS and race-horses never last long.

———

IT is a poor sport that is not worth the candle.

———

HE that is fallen cannot help him that is down.

———

EVERY one is witty for his own purpose.

———

A little let* lets an ill workman.

———

GOOD workmen are seldom rich.

———

By doing nothing we learn to do ill.

———oo§o§oo———

A GREAT dowry is a bed full of brambles.

———oo§o§oo———

No profit to honor, no honor to religion.

———oo§o§oo———

EVERY sin brings its punishment with it.

———oo§o§oo———

OF him that speaks ill, consider the life more than the word.

———oo§o§oo———

You cannot hide an eel in a sack.

———oo§o§oo———

GIVE not Saint Peter so much, to leave Saint Paul nothing.

———oo§o§oo———

You cannot flay* a stone.

———oo§o§oo———

THE chief disease that reigns this year is folly.

———oo§o§oo———

A SLEEPY master makes his servant a lout.*

———oo§o§oo———

BETTER speak truth rudely than lie covertly.

———oo§o§oo———

HE that fears leaves, let him not go into the wood.

———oo§o§oo———

ONE foot is better than two crutches.

———oo§o§oo———

BETTER suffer ill than do ill.

———oo꞉ʘ꞉oo———

NEITHER praise nor dispraise thyself: thy actions serve the turn.

———oo꞉ʘ꞉oo———

SOFT and fair goes far.

———oo꞉ʘ꞉oo———

THE constancy of the benefit of the year in their seasons
argues a Deity.

———oo꞉ʘ꞉oo———

PRAISE none too much, for all are fickle.

———oo꞉ʘ꞉oo———

IT is absurd to warm one in his armor.

———oo꞉ʘ꞉oo———

LAWSUITS consume time, and money, and rest, and friends.

———oo꞉ʘ꞉oo———

NATURE draws more than ten teams.

———oo꞉ʘ꞉oo———

HE that has a wife and children wants not business.

———oo꞉ʘ꞉oo———

A ship and a woman are ever repairing.

———oo꞉ʘ꞉oo———

HE that fears death lives not.

———oo꞉ʘ꞉oo———

HE that pities another remembers himself.

———oo꞉ʘ꞉oo———

HE that does what he should not, shall feel what he would not.

———◦◦◦◦◦◦———

HE that marries for wealth sells his liberty.

———◦◦◦◦◦◦———

HE that once hits is ever bending.

———◦◦◦◦◦◦———

HE that serves must serve.

———◦◦◦◦◦◦———

HE that lends gives.

———◦◦◦◦◦◦———

HE that preacheth giveth alms.

———◦◦◦◦◦◦———

HE that cockers* his child provides for his enemy.

———◦◦◦◦◦◦———

A PITIFUL look asks enough.

———◦◦◦◦◦◦———

WHO will sell the cow must say the word.

———◦◦◦◦◦◦———

SERVICE is no inheritance.

———◦◦◦◦◦◦———

THE faulty stands on his guard.

———◦◦◦◦◦◦———

A KINSMAN, a friend, or whom you entreat, take not to serve you if you will be served neatly.

———◦◦◦◦◦◦———

AT court every one for himself.

————ooჰ◎ჰoo————

To a crafty man a crafty and a half.

————ooჰ◎ჰoo————

HE that is thrown would ever wrestle.

————ooჰ◎ჰoo————

HE that serves well need not ask his wages.

————ooჰ◎ჰoo————

FAIR language grates not the tongue.

————ooჰ◎ჰoo————

A GOOD heart cannot lie.

————ooჰ◎ჰoo————

GOOD swimmers at length are drowned.

————ooჰ◎ჰoo————

GOOD land, evil way.

————ooჰ◎ჰoo————

IN doing we learn.

————ooჰ◎ჰoo————

IT is good walking with a horse in one's hand.

————ooჰ◎ჰoo————

GOD, and parents, and our master, can never be requited.

————ooჰ◎ჰoo————

AN ill deed cannot bring honor.

————ooჰ◎ჰoo————

A SMALL heart has small desires.

————ooჰ◎ჰoo————

ALL are not merry that dance lightly.

COURTESY on one side only lasts not long.

WINE counsels seldom prosper.

WEENING* is not measure.

THE best of the sport is to do the deed, and say nothing.

IF thou thyself canst do it, attend no other's help or hand.

OF a little thing, a little displeaseth.

HE warms too near that burns.

GOD keep me from four houses: a usurer's, a tavern, a spital,* and a prison.

IN a hundred ells* of contention, there is not an inch of love.

DO what thou oughtest, and come what come can.

HUNGER makes dinners, pastime suppers.

In a long journey straw weighs.

———∘∘⚬⚬⚬∘∘———

Women laugh when they can, and weep when they will.

———∘∘⚬⚬⚬∘∘———

War is death's feast.

———∘∘⚬⚬⚬∘∘———

Set good against evil.

———∘∘⚬⚬⚬∘∘———

He that brings good news knocks hard.

———∘∘⚬⚬⚬∘∘———

Beat the dog before the lion.

———∘∘⚬⚬⚬∘∘———

Haste comes not alone.

———∘∘⚬⚬⚬∘∘———

You must lose a fly to catch a trout.

———∘∘⚬⚬⚬∘∘———

No prison is fair, nor love foul.

———∘∘⚬⚬⚬∘∘———

He is not free that draws his chain.

———∘∘⚬⚬⚬∘∘———

He goes not out of his way that goes to a good inn.

———∘∘⚬⚬⚬∘∘———

There comes nought out of the sack but what was there.

———∘∘⚬⚬⚬∘∘———

A little given seasonably excuses a great gift.

———∘∘⚬⚬⚬∘∘———

HE looks not well to himself that looks not ever.

———∘ο⦂⊚⦂ο∘———

HE thinks not well that thinks not again.

———∘ο⦂⊚⦂ο∘———

RELIGION, credit, and the eye are not to be touched.

———∘ο⦂⊚⦂ο∘———

THE tongue is not steel, yet it cuts.

———∘ο⦂⊚⦂ο∘———

A WHITE wall is the paper of a fool.

———∘ο⦂⊚⦂ο∘———

THEY talk of Christmas so long that it comes.

———∘ο⦂⊚⦂ο∘———

THAT is gold which is worth gold.

———∘ο⦂⊚⦂ο∘———

IT is good tying the sack before it be full.

———∘ο⦂⊚⦂ο∘———

WORDS are women, deeds are men.

———∘ο⦂⊚⦂ο∘———

POVERTY is no sin.

———∘ο⦂⊚⦂ο∘———

A STONE in a well is not lost.

———∘ο⦂⊚⦂ο∘———

HE can give little to his servant that licks his knife.

———∘ο⦂⊚⦂ο∘———

PROMISING is the eve of giving.

———∘ο⦂⊚⦂ο∘———

HE that keeps his own makes war.

———∘∘⦂◉⦂∘∘———

THE wolf must die in his own skin.

———∘∘⦂◉⦂∘∘———

GOODS are theirs that enjoy them.

———∘∘⦂◉⦂∘∘———

HE that sends a fool expects one.

———∘∘⦂◉⦂∘∘———

HE that can stay obtains.

———∘∘⦂◉⦂∘∘———

HE that gains well and spends well needs no account book.

———∘∘⦂◉⦂∘∘———

HE that endures is not overcome.

———∘∘⦂◉⦂∘∘———

HE that gives all before he dies provides to suffer.

———∘∘⦂◉⦂∘∘———

HE that talks much of his happiness summons grief.

———∘∘⦂◉⦂∘∘———

HE that loves the tree loves the branch.

———∘∘⦂◉⦂∘∘———

WHO hastens a glutton chokes him.

———∘∘⦂◉⦂∘∘———

WHO praiseth Saint Peter, does not blame Saint Paul.

———∘∘⦂◉⦂∘∘———

HE that has not the craft, let him shut up shop.

———∘∘⦂◉⦂∘∘———

HE that knows nothing doubts nothing.

———◦○ॐ○◦———

GREEN wood makes a hot fire.

———◦○ॐ○◦———

HE that marries late marries ill.

———◦○ॐ○◦———

HE that passeth a winter's day escapes an enemy.

———◦○ॐ○◦———

THE rich knows not who is his friend.

———◦○ॐ○◦———

A MORNING sun, and a wine-bred child, and a Latin-bred woman, seldom end well.

———◦○ॐ○◦———

To a close shorn sheep God gives wind by measure.

———◦○ॐ○◦———

A PLEASURE long expected is dear enough sold.

———◦○ॐ○◦———

A POOR man's cow dies a rich man's child.

———◦○ॐ○◦———

THE cow knows not what her tail is worth till she has lost it.

———◦○ॐ○◦———

CHOOSE a horse made, and a wife to make.

———◦○ॐ○◦———

IT is an ill air where we gain nothing.

———◦○ॐ○◦———

HE has not lived that lives not after death.

———⚬⚬⚬⚬———

SO many men in court, and so many strangers.

———⚬⚬⚬⚬———

HE quits his place well that leaves his friend there.

———⚬⚬⚬⚬———

THAT which sufficeth is not little.

———⚬⚬⚬⚬———

GOOD news may be told at any time, but ill in the morning.

———⚬⚬⚬⚬———

HE that would be a gentleman, let him go to an assault.

———⚬⚬⚬⚬———

WHO pays the physician does the cure.

———⚬⚬⚬⚬———

NONE knows the weight of another's burden.

———⚬⚬⚬⚬———

EVERY one has a fool in his sleeve.

———⚬⚬⚬⚬———

ONE hour's sleep before midnight is worth three after.

———⚬⚬⚬⚬———

IN a retreat the lame are foremost.

———⚬⚬⚬⚬———

IT is more pain to do nothing than something.

———⚬⚬⚬⚬———

AMONGST good men two men suffice.

———⚬⚬⚬⚬———

THERE needs a long time to know the world's pulse.

———o·o¿·○¿·oo———

THE offspring of those that are very young or very old last not.

———o·o¿·○¿·oo———

A TYRANT is most tyrant to himself.

———o·o¿·○¿·oo———

Too much taking heed is loss.

———o·o¿·○¿·oo———

CRAFT against craft makes no living.

———o·o¿·○¿·oo———

THE reverend are ever before.

———o·o¿·○¿·oo———

FRANCE is a meadow that cuts thrice a year.

———o·o¿·○¿·oo———

IT is easier to build two chimneys than to maintain one.

———o·o¿·○¿·oo———

THE court has no almanac.

———o·o¿·○¿·oo———

HE that will enter into Paradise must have a good key.

———o·o¿·○¿·oo———

WHEN you enter into a house leave the anger ever at the door.

———o·o¿·○¿·oo———

HE has no leisure who uses it not.

———o·o¿·○¿·oo———

IT is a wicked thing to make a dearth one's garner.

———o·o¿·○¿·oo———

HE that deals in the world needs four sieves.

———❧———

TAKE heed of an ox before, of a horse behind, of a monk on all sides.

———❧———

THE year does nothing else but open and shut.

———❧———

THE ignorant has an eagle's wings and an owl's eyes.

———❧———

THERE are more physicians in health than drunkards.

———❧———

THE wife is the key of the house.

———❧———

THE law is not the same at morning and at night.

———❧———

WAR and physic are governed by the eye.

———❧———

HALF the world knows not how the other half lives.

———❧———

DEATH keeps no calendar.

———❧———

SHIPS fear fire more than water.

———❧———

THE least foolish is wise.

———❧———

THE chief box of health is time.

———∘∘ɞ◉ʚ∘∘———

SILKS and satins put out the fire in the chimney.

———∘∘ɞ◉ʚ∘∘———

THE first blow is as much as two.

———∘∘ɞ◉ʚ∘∘———

THE life of man is a winter way.

———∘∘ɞ◉ʚ∘∘———

THE way is an ill neighbor.

———∘∘ɞ◉ʚ∘∘———

AN old man's staff is the rapper of death's door.

———∘∘ɞ◉ʚ∘∘———

LIFE is half spent before we know what it is.

———∘∘ɞ◉ʚ∘∘———

THE singing man keeps his shop in his throat.

———∘∘ɞ◉ʚ∘∘———

THE body is more dressed than the soul.

———∘∘ɞ◉ʚ∘∘———

THE body is sooner dressed than the soul.

———∘∘ɞ◉ʚ∘∘———

THE physician owes all to the patient, but the patient owes
nothing to him but a little money.

———∘∘ɞ◉ʚ∘∘———

THE little cannot be great unless he devour many.

———∘∘ɞ◉ʚ∘∘———

TIME undermines us.

———∘∘⟡∘∘———

THE choleric drinks, the melancholic eats, the phlegmatic sleeps.

———∘∘⟡∘∘———

THE apothecary's mortar spoils the luter's music.

———∘∘⟡∘∘———

CONVERSATION makes one what he is.

———∘∘⟡∘∘———

THE deaf gains the injury.

———∘∘⟡∘∘———

YEARS know more than books.

———∘∘⟡∘∘———

WINE is a turncoat, first a friend, then an enemy.

———∘∘⟡∘∘———

WINE ever pays for his lodging.

———∘∘⟡∘∘———

WINE makes all sorts of creatures at table.

———∘∘⟡∘∘———

WINE that cost nothing is digested before it be drunk.

———∘∘⟡∘∘———

TREES eat but once.

———∘∘⟡∘∘———

ARMOR is light at table.

———∘∘⟡∘∘———

GOOD horses make short miles.

———∘∘⟡∘∘———

CASTLES are forests of stones.

———⚬⚬⚬———

THE dainties of the great are the tears of the poor.

———⚬⚬⚬———

PARSONS are souls' waggoners.

———⚬⚬⚬———

CHILDREN when they are little make parents fools, when they are great they make them mad.

———⚬⚬⚬———

THE master absent, and the house dead.

———⚬⚬⚬———

DOGS are fine in the field.

———⚬⚬⚬———

SINS are not known till they be acted.

———⚬⚬⚬———

THORNS whiten, yet do nothing.

———⚬⚬⚬———

ALL are presumed good till they are found in a fault.

———⚬⚬⚬———

THE great put the little on the hook.

———⚬⚬⚬———

THE great would have none great, and the little all little.

———⚬⚬⚬———

THE Italians are wise before the deed, the Germans in the deed, the French after the deed.

———⚬⚬⚬———

EVERY mile is two in winter.

———oo⳼◉⳼oo———

SPECTACLES are death's arquebuse.*

———oo⳼◉⳼oo———

LAWYERS' houses are built on the heads of fools.

———oo⳼◉⳼oo———

THE house is a fine house when good folks are within.

———oo⳼◉⳼oo———

THE best bred have the best portion.

———oo⳼◉⳼oo———

THE first and last frosts are the worst.

———oo⳼◉⳼oo———

GIFTS enter everywhere without a wimble.

———oo⳼◉⳼oo———

PRINCES have no way.

———oo⳼◉⳼oo———

KNOWLEDGE makes one laugh, but wealth makes one dance.

———oo⳼◉⳼oo———

THE citizen is at his business before he rise.

———oo⳼◉⳼oo———

THE eyes have one language everywhere.

———oo⳼◉⳼oo———

IT is better to have wings than horns.

———oo⳼◉⳼oo———

BETTER be a fool than a knave.*

———oo⳼◉⳼oo———

COUNT not four, except you have them in a wallet.

———⚬⚬⊙⚬⚬———

To live peaceably with all breeds good blood.

———⚬⚬⊙⚬⚬———

YOU may be on land, yet not in a garden.

———⚬⚬⊙⚬⚬———

YOU cannot make the fire so low but it will get out.

———⚬⚬⊙⚬⚬———

WE know not who lives or dies.

———⚬⚬⊙⚬⚬———

MUCH money makes a country poor, for it sets a dearer price on everything.

———⚬⚬⊙⚬⚬———

THERE is nobody will go to hell for company.

———⚬⚬⊙⚬⚬———

THE devil never assails a man except he finds him either void of knowledge, or of the fear of God.

———⚬⚬⊙⚬⚬———

WE bachelors laugh and show our teeth, but you married men laugh till your hearts ache.

———⚬⚬⊙⚬⚬———

CIVIL wars of France make a million of atheists and thirty thousand witches.

———⚬⚬⊙⚬⚬———

HERE is a talk of the Turk and the Pope, but my next neighbor does me more harm than either of them both.

———⚬⚬⊙⚬⚬———

AN ox is taken by the horns, and a man by the tongue.

———∘∘⦂⦂∘∘———

MANY things are lost for want of asking.

———∘∘⦂⦂∘∘———

No churchyard is so handsome, that a man would desire
straight to be buried there.

———∘∘⦂⦂∘∘———

CITIES are taken by the ears.

———∘∘⦂⦂∘∘———

ONCE a year a man may say, On his conscience.

———∘∘⦂⦂∘∘———

WE leave more to do when we die than we have done.

———∘∘⦂⦂∘∘———

WITH customs we live well, but laws undo us.

———∘∘⦂⦂∘∘———

To speak of a usurer at the table mars the wine.

———∘∘⦂⦂∘∘———

PAINS to get, care to keep, fear to lose.

———∘∘⦂⦂∘∘———

FOR a morning rain leave not your journey.

———∘∘⦂⦂∘∘———

ONE fair day in winter makes not birds merry.

———∘∘⦂⦂∘∘———

HE that learns a trade has a purchase made.

———∘∘⦂⦂∘∘———

WHEN all men have what belongs to them it cannot be much.

———oo｝⊚｝oo———

THOUGH God take the sun out of the heaven, yet we must have patience.

———oo｝⊚｝oo———

WHEN a man sleeps his head is in his stomach.

———oo｝⊚｝oo———

WHEN one is on horseback he knows all things.

———oo｝⊚｝oo———

WHEN God is made master of a family, He orders the disorderly.

———oo｝⊚｝oo———

WHEN a lackey comes to hell's door, the devils lock the gates.

———oo｝⊚｝oo———

HE that is at ease seeks dainties.

———oo｝⊚｝oo———

HE that has charge of souls transports them not in bundles.

———oo｝⊚｝oo———

HE that tells his wife news is but newly married.

———oo｝⊚｝oo———

HE that is in a town in May loseth his spring.

———oo｝⊚｝oo———

HE that is in a tavern, thinks he is in a vine-garden.

———oo｝⊚｝oo———

HE that praiseth himself spattereth himself.

———oo｝⊚｝oo———

HE that is a master must serve (another).

————◦◦⟡◉⟡◦◦————

HE that is surprised with the first frost feels it all the winter after.

————◦◦⟡◉⟡◦◦————

HE a beast does die that has done no good to his country.

————◦◦⟡◉⟡◦◦————

HE that follows the Lord hopes to go before.

————◦◦⟡◉⟡◦◦————

HE that dies without the company of good men puts not himself into a good way.

————◦◦⟡◉⟡◦◦————

WHO has no head needs no heart.

————◦◦⟡◉⟡◦◦————

WHO has no haste in his business, mountains to him seem valleys.

————◦◦⟡◉⟡◦◦————

SPEAK not of my debts, unless you mean to pay them.

————◦◦⟡◉⟡◦◦————

HE that is not in the wars is not out of danger.

————◦◦⟡◉⟡◦◦————

HE that gives me small gifts, would have me live.

————◦◦⟡◉⟡◦◦————

HE that is his own counsellor knows nothing sure but what he has laid out.

————◦◦⟡◉⟡◦◦————

HE that has lands has quarrels.

———∘○⁖⊚⁖○∘———

HE that goes to bed thirsty riseth healthy.

———∘○⁖⊚⁖○∘———

WHO will make a door of gold must knock a nail everyday.

———∘○⁖⊚⁖○∘———

A trade is better than service.

———∘○⁖⊚⁖○∘———

HE that lives in hope danceth without music.

———∘○⁖⊚⁖○∘———

To review one's store is to mow twice.

———∘○⁖⊚⁖○∘———

SAINT Luke was a saint and a physician, yet is dead.

———∘○⁖⊚⁖○∘———

WITHOUT business, debauchery.

———∘○⁖⊚⁖○∘———

WITHOUT danger we cannot get beyond danger.

———∘○⁖⊚⁖○∘———

IF gold knew what gold is, gold would get gold, I wis.*

———∘○⁖⊚⁖○∘———

HEALTH and sickness surely are men's double enemies.

———∘○⁖⊚⁖○∘———

LITTLE losses amaze, great tame.

———∘○⁖⊚⁖○∘———

CHOOSE none for thy servants who have served thy betters.

———∘○⁖⊚⁖○∘———

SERVICE without reward is punishment.

———∘∘ː◎ː∘∘———

IF the husband be not at home, there is nobody.

———∘∘ː◎ː∘∘———

AN oath that is not to be made is not to be kept.

———∘∘ː◎ː∘∘———

THE eye is bigger than the belly.

———∘∘ː◎ː∘∘———

IF you would be at ease, all the world is not.

———∘∘ː◎ː∘∘———

WERE it not for the bone in the leg, all the world would turn carpenters (to make them crutches).

———∘∘ː◎ː∘∘———

IF you must fly, fly well.

———∘∘ː◎ː∘∘———

ALL that shakes falls not.

———∘∘ː◎ː∘∘———

ALL beasts of prey are strong or treacherous.

———∘∘ː◎ː∘∘———

IF the brain sows not corn, it plants thistles.

———∘∘ː◎ː∘∘———

A MAN well mounted is ever choleric.

———∘∘ː◎ː∘∘———

EVERY one is a master and servant.

———∘∘ː◎ː∘∘———

A PIECE of a churchyard fits everybody.

———∘⚬⟨◉⟩⚬∘———

ONE mouth does nothing without another.

———∘⚬⟨◉⟩⚬∘———

A MASTER of straw eats a servant of steel.

———∘⚬⟨◉⟩⚬∘———

AN old cat sports not with her prey.

———∘⚬⟨◉⟩⚬∘———

A WOMAN conceals what she knows not.

———∘⚬⟨◉⟩⚬∘———

HE that wipes the child's nose kisseth the mother's cheek.

———∘⚬⟨◉⟩⚬∘———

GENTILITY is nothing but ancient riches.

———∘⚬⟨◉⟩⚬∘———

To go upon the Franciscans' hackney;* *i.e.* on foot.

———∘⚬⟨◉⟩⚬∘———

AMIENS was taken by the fox, and retaken by the lion.

———∘⚬⟨◉⟩⚬∘———

AFTER death the doctor.

———∘⚬⟨◉⟩⚬∘———

READY money is a ready medicine.

———∘⚬⟨◉⟩⚬∘———

IT is the philosophy of the distaff.

———∘⚬⟨◉⟩⚬∘———

To go where the king goes afoot; *i.e.* to the stool.

———∘⚬⟨◉⟩⚬∘———

IT is a sheep of Beery, it is marked on the nose (applied to those that have a blow).

————ooᵔ⊙ᵔoo————

To build castles in Spain.

————ooᵔ⊙ᵔoo————

AN idle youth, a needy age.

————ooᵔ⊙ᵔoo————

SILK doth quench the fire in the kitchen.

————ooᵔ⊙ᵔoo————

THE words ending in "ique" do mock the physician; as hectique, paralitique, apoplectique, lethargique.

————ooᵔ⊙ᵔoo————

HE that trusts much obliges much, says the Spaniard.

————ooᵔ⊙ᵔoo————

HE that thinks amiss concludes worse.

————ooᵔ⊙ᵔoo————

A MAN would live in Italy (a place of pleasure), but he would choose to die in Spain (where they say the Catholic religion is professed with greatest strictness).

————ooᵔ⊙ᵔoo————

WHATSOEVER was the father of a disease, an ill diet was the mother.

————ooᵔ⊙ᵔoo————

FRENZY, heresy, and jealousy, seldom cured.

————ooᵔ⊙ᵔoo————

BETTER a snotty child than his nose wiped off.

————ooᵔ⊙ᵔoo————

THERE is no heat of affection but is joined with some idleness of brain, says the Spaniard.

———oo⊱⊰oo———

THE war is not done so long as my enemy lives.

———oo⊱⊰oo———

SOME evils are cured by contempt.

———oo⊱⊰oo———

POWER seldom grows old at court.

———oo⊱⊰oo———

DANGER itself is the best remedy for danger.

———oo⊱⊰oo———

FAVOR will as surely perish as life.

———oo⊱⊰oo———

FEAR the beadle* of the law.

———oo⊱⊰oo———

HERESY is the school of pride.

———oo⊱⊰oo———

FOR the same man to be a heretic and a good subject is impossible.

———oo⊱⊰oo———

HERESY may be easier kept out than shook off.

———oo⊱⊰oo———

INFANTS' manners are molded more by the example of parents than by stars at their nativities.

———oo⊱⊰oo———

MARRY your daughters betimes* lest they marry themselves.

———oo⊱⊰oo———

THEY favor learning whose actions are worthy of a learned pen.

———∘∘⟡∘∘———

MODESTY sets off one newly come to honor.

———∘∘⟡∘∘———

NO naked man is sought after to be rifled.

———∘∘⟡∘∘———

THERE is no such conquering weapon as the necessity
of conquering.

———∘∘⟡∘∘———

NOTHING secure unless suspected.

———∘∘⟡∘∘———

NO tie can oblige the perfidious.

———∘∘⟡∘∘———

SPIES are the ears and eyes of princes.

———∘∘⟡∘∘———

THE life of spies is to know, not be known.

———∘∘⟡∘∘———

RELIGION a stalking horse to shoot other fowl.

———∘∘⟡∘∘———

IT is a dangerous fire begins in the bed-straw.

———∘∘⟡∘∘———

COVETOUSNESS breaks the bag.

———∘∘⟡∘∘———

FEAR keeps and looks to the vineyard, and not the owner.

———∘∘⟡∘∘———

THE noise is greater than the nuts.

——◦○ː◎ː○◦——

TWO sparrows on one ear of corn make an ill agreement.

——◦○ː◎ː○◦——

THE world is nowadays, God save the conqueror.

——◦○ː◎ː○◦——

UNSOUND minds, like unsound bodies, if you feed, you poison.

——◦○ː◎ː○◦——

NOT only ought fortune to be pictured on a wheel, but
everything else in this world.

——◦○ː◎ː○◦——

ALL covet, all lose.

——◦○ː◎ː○◦——

BETTER is one *Accipe,** than twice to say, *Dabo tibi.**

——◦○ː◎ː○◦——

AN ass endures his burden, but not more than his burden.

——◦○ː◎ː○◦——

THREATENED men eat bread, says the Spaniard.

——◦○ː◎ː○◦——

THE beads in the hand, and the devil in capuch (or cape of
the cloak).

——◦○ː◎ː○◦——

HE that will do thee a good turn, either he will be gone or die.

——◦○ː◎ː○◦——

I escaped the thunder, and fell into the lightning.

——◦○ː◎ː○◦——

A man of a great memory, without learning, has a rock and a spindle, and no staff to spin.

———⊶⊷———

THE death of wolves is the safety of the sheep.

———⊶⊷———

HE that is once born once must die.

———⊶⊷———

HE that has but one eye must be afraid to lose it.

———⊶⊷———

HE that makes himself a sheep shall be eat by the wolf.

———⊶⊷———

HE that steals an egg will steal an ox.

———⊶⊷———

HE that will be surety shall pay.

———⊶⊷———

HE that is afraid of leaves goes not to the wood.

———⊶⊷———

IN the mouth of a bad dog falls often a good bone.

———⊶⊷———

THOSE that God loves do not live long.

———⊶⊷———

STILL fisheth he that catcheth one.

———⊶⊷———

ALL flesh is not venison.

———⊶⊷———

A city that parleys* is half gotten.

———o○¿◎¿o○———

A dead bee makes no honey.

———o○¿◎¿o○———

An old dog barks not in vain.

———o○¿◎¿o○———

They that hold the greatest farms pay the least rent (applied to rich men that are unthankful to God).

———o○¿◎¿o○———

Old camels carry young camels' skins to the market.

———o○¿◎¿o○———

He that has time and looks for better time, time comes that he repents himself of time.

———o○¿◎¿o○———

Words and feathers the wind carries away.

———o○¿◎¿o○———

Of a pig's tail you can never make a good shaft.

———o○¿◎¿o○———

The bath of the blackamoor* has sworn not to whiten.

———o○¿◎¿o○———

To a greedy-eating horse a short halter.

———o○¿◎¿o○———

The devil divides the world between atheism and superstition.

———o○¿◎¿o○———

Such a saint, such an offering.

———o○¿◎¿o○———

WE do it soon enough, if that we do be well.

———ooᣚⓄᣚoo———

CRUELTY is more cruel, if we defer the pain.

———ooᣚⓄᣚoo———

WHAT one day gives us another takes away from us.

———ooᣚⓄᣚoo———

To seek in a sheep five feet when there are but four.

———ooᣚⓄᣚoo———

A scabbed horse cannot abide the comb.

———ooᣚⓄᣚoo———

GOD strikes with His finger, and not with all His arm.

———ooᣚⓄᣚoo———

GOD gives His wrath by weight, and without weight His mercy.

———ooᣚⓄᣚoo———

OF a new prince new bondage.

———ooᣚⓄᣚoo———

NEW things are fair.

———ooᣚⓄᣚoo———

FORTUNE to one is mother, to another is stepmother.

———ooᣚⓄᣚoo———

THERE is no man, though never so little, but sometimes he
can hurt.

———ooᣚⓄᣚoo———

THE horse that draws after him his halter is not altogether
escaped.

———ooᣚⓄᣚoo———

WE must recoil a little, to the end we may leap the better.

———o○;○;○o———

No love is foul nor prison fair.

———o○;○;○o———

No day so clear but has dark clouds.

———o○;○;○o———

No hare so small but has his shadow.

———o○;○;○o———

A wolf will never make war against another wolf.

———o○;○;○o———

WE must love, as looking one day to hate.

———o○;○;○o———

IT is good to have some friends both in heaven and hell.

———o○;○;○o———

IT is very hard to shave an egg.

———o○;○;○o———

IT is good to hold the ass by the bridle.

———o○;○;○o———

THE healthful man can give counsel to the sick.

———o○;○;○o———

THE death of a young wolf does never come too soon.

———o○;○;○o———

THE rage of a wild boar is able to spoil more than one wood.

———o○;○;○o———

VIRTUE flies from the heart of a mercenary man.

———o○;○;○o———

THE wolf eats oft of the sheep that have been warned.

———∘∘⟡∘∘———

THE mouse that has but one hole is quickly taken.

———∘∘⟡∘∘———

To play at chess when the house is on fire.

———∘∘⟡∘∘———

THE itch of disputing is the scab of the church.

———∘∘⟡∘∘———

FOLLOW not truth too near the heels, lest it dash out thy teeth.

———∘∘⟡∘∘———

EITHER wealth is much increased, or moderation is
much decayed.

———∘∘⟡∘∘———

SAY to pleasure, "Gentle *Eve*, I will none of your apple."

———∘∘⟡∘∘———

WHEN war begins, then hell openeth.

———∘∘⟡∘∘———

THERE is a remedy for everything, could men find it.

———∘∘⟡∘∘———

THERE is an hour wherein a man might be happy all his life
could he find it.

———∘∘⟡∘∘———

GREAT fortune brings with it great misfortune.

———∘∘⟡∘∘———

A fair day in winter is the mother of a storm.

———∘∘⟡∘∘———

WOE be to him that reads but one book.

———oₒ⁍⊙⁍ₒ○———

TITHE, and be rich.

———oₒ⁍⊙⁍ₒ○———

THE wrath of a mighty man, and
the tumult of the people.

———oₒ⁍⊙⁍ₒ○———

MAD folks in a narrow place.

———oₒ⁍⊙⁍ₒ○———

CREDIT decayed, and people that
have nothing.

———oₒ⁍⊙⁍ₒ○———

Take
heed
of

A YOUNG wench, a prophetess,
and a Latin-bred woman.

———oₒ⁍⊙⁍ₒ○———

A PERSON marked, and
a widow thrice married.

———oₒ⁍⊙⁍ₒ○———

FOUL dirty ways and long sickness.

———oₒ⁍⊙⁍ₒ○———

WIND that comes in at a hole,
and a reconciled enemy.

———oₒ⁍⊙⁍ₒ○———

A STEP-MOTHER; the very name
of her sufficeth.

———oₒ⁍⊙⁍ₒ○———

PRINCES are venison in heaven.

———○○⦂◎⦂○○———

CRITICS are like brushers of noblemen's clothes.

———○○⦂◎⦂○○———

HE is a great necromancer, for he asks counsel of the dead, *i.e.* books.

———○○⦂◎⦂○○———

A MAN is known to be mortal by two things: sleep and lust.

———○○⦂◎⦂○○———

"LOVE without end, has no end," says the Spaniard; meaning, "if it were not begun on particular ends it would last."

———○○⦂◎⦂○○———

STAY awhile that we may make an end the sooner.

———○○⦂◎⦂○○———

PRESENTS of love fear not to be ill taken of strangers.

———○○⦂◎⦂○○———

To seek these things is lost labor: geese in an oil pot, fat hogs among Jews, and wine in a fishing net.

———○○⦂◎⦂○○———

SOME men plant an opinion they seem to eradicate.

———○○⦂◎⦂○○———

THE philosophy of princes is to dive into the secrets of men, leaving the secrets of nature to those that have spare time.

———○○⦂◎⦂○○———

STATES have their conversions and periods as well as natural bodies.

———○○⦂◎⦂○○———

GREAT deservers grow intolerable presumers.

————◦◦°◌°◦◦————

THE love of money and the love of learning rarely meet.

————◦◦°◌°◦◦————

TRUST no friend with that you need, fear him as if he were your enemy.

————◦◦°◌°◦◦————

SOME had rather lose their friend than their jest.

GLOSSARY

(Words are marked with an asterisk in the text.)

Accipe—Latin for "accept, take, receive."

Ague—The cold fit which precedes a fever, or a paroxysm of fever in intermittents. It is accompanied with shivering.

Arquebuse—A sort of hand gun or firearm a contrivance answering to a trigger, by which the burning match was applied.

Bauble—The fool or jester carried in his hand a wooden scepter called a bauble. It was a short stick ornamented at the end with the figure of a fool's head, or with that of a puppet or doll.

Beadle—A messenger or crier of a court; a servitor; one who cites persons to appear and answer.

Betimes—Seasonably; in good season or time; before it is late.

Blackamoor—A person with dark skin, a negro.

Brabble—To clamor; to contest noisily.

Clack—To make a sudden sharp noise, as by striking or cracking; to clink; to click.

Cocker—To fondle; to indulge; to treat with tenderness; to pamper.

Comfit—A dry sweetmeat; any kind of fruit, root, or seed preserved with sugar and dried; a confection.

Dabo tibi—Latin for "I will give you."

Ell—A measure of different lengths in different countries, used chiefly for measuring cloth.

Escurial—A palace and mausoleum of the kinds of Spain, being a vast and wonderful structure about twenty-five miles northwest of Madrid.

Flay—To take off the skin or surface of any thing.

Groundsel—A plant of the genus Senecio, of several species.

Hackney—A horse kept for hire; a horse much used.

Half-man—a weak man; reduced or diminished.

Halter—A rope for hanging malefactors; strong cord or string.

Knave—1. A boy; a man-child. 2. A servant. 3. A false deceitful fellow; a dishonest man or boy.

Lanthorn—a lantern.

Let—To retard; to hinder; to impede; to interpose obstructions.

Lout—A mean awkward fellow; a bumpkin; a clown.

Mora—delay, postponement.

Parley—To confer with on some point of mutual concern; to discuss orally; hence, to confer with an enemy.

Rheum—A thin serous fluid, secreted by the mucous glands, especially from the eyes or nose.

Spital or spittle—Corrupted from hospital; a charity hospital.

Strumpet—female prostitute.

Trencher—A wooden plate. Trenchers were in use among the common people of New England till the revolution.

Ward—To guard; to deep in safety; to watch.

Ween—To think; to imagine; to fancy.

Wis—To think; to suppose; to imagine.

APPENDIX

It has been objected that there is no absolute proof that the proverbs were translated by Herbert (see "Notes and Queries," second series, No. 57, p. 88), but these objections were ably set aside by Mr. Mayor in the same series, p. 130. It appears that Herbert's works were held in high esteem and kept in MS. at Little Gidding, from whence Dr. John Mapletoft derived his two MS. collections of proverbs, one of which professed to be a work of Herbert's. There is, therefore, little reason to doubt that he was the translator and editor of them.[1] (See the reprint of this entire discussion below.)

QUERIES—WAS GEORGE HERBERT THE COMPILER OF "JACULA PRUDENTUM, OR OUTLANDISH PROVERBS," ETC.?

For two centuries this work has been circulated with the venerated name of George Herbert, so that to question its authenticity at this late period may perhaps be thought hypercritical. Its literary history, however, is so very obscure, that it seems

---

1 *The Works of George Herbert in Poetry and Prose*, (New York: John Wurtele Lovell, 1881), p. 437.

expedient to elicit the opinions of the readers of "N. & Q." respecting it, among whom will doubtless be found many a lover of "the sweet singer of the Temple."

The first edition appeared eight years after Herbert's death with the following title:

"Outlandish Proverbs, selected by Mr. G. H.[1] London, Printed by T. P. for Humphrey Blunden, at the Castle in Corn-hill. 1640. 12mo."

This edition consists of 1032 Proverbs, all numbered. Copies of it are in the Bodleian and Grenville libraries. The words, "By Mr. G. H.," are obliterated with a pen in the Bodleian copy! This correction has been noticed by the compilers of the Bodleian Catalogue, as they have entered the work under *Proverbia*, and not under the initials G. H., which they have also suppressed.

The second edition, with the name in full, appeared in 1651, eleven years after the first edition, and nineteen after the death of George Herbert. This edition is entitled,

"Jacula Prudentum: or Outlandish Proverbs, Sentences, etc. Selected by Mr. George Herbert, late Orator of the University of Cambridge, London, Printed by T. Maxey for T. Garthwait, at the little North door of St. Paul's. 1651. 12mo."

This book contains 1190 Proverbs, but unnumbered; and these make 70 pages. Then follow some miscellaneous articles commencing with page 171 (!), as if part of some other work. These addenda are—

"1. The Author's Prayers before and after Sermon.

---

1 The initials G. H. were those of two other celebrated living writers at this time, namely, George Hakewill and George Hughes. Sea *Bodleian Catalogue*. vol. ii, p. 222.

2. Mr. G. Herbert to Master N. F. [Nicholas Ferrar] upon the translation of Valdesso.

3. Lines in Memory of Lord Bacon, and to Dr. Donne.

4. An Addition of Apothegms by several Authors."

Nos. 2 and 3 are the undoubted productions of Herbert. But on a careful examination of the contents of this volume the suspicion naturally arises that it may be a spurious production; in fact, the work forcibly reminds one of Curll's miscellaneous volumes.

It must be remembered, that in the following year, 1652, Barnabas Oley, the editor of *A Priest to the Temple, or the Country Parson*, published the first edition of that work, with his Life of Herbert; but neither in this nor in the two subsequent editions which passed under his eye[1] do we find the "Prayers before and after Sermon," which are placed at the end of the *Country Parson* in all the later editions, excepting the reprint in *The Clergyman's Instructor*, Oxford, 1827. When it is remembered how punctiliously George Herbert walked according to canonical rule in small as well as in great matters, it seems highly improbable that he would use these two unauthorized prayers in Divine service. Walton tells us, that when Mr. Duncon visited Herbert in his last illness, Herbert said to him,—

"Sir, I see by your habit that you are a priest, and I desire you to pray with me: which being granted, Mr. Duncon asked him, What prayers? To which Mr. Herbert's answer was, 'O Sir! the prayers of my Mother, the Church of England: *no other prayers are equal to them!* But at this

1 Oley's *Life of Herbert* first appeared in 1652, with additions in 1671 and 1675. Walton's *Life of Herbert* was first published in 1670. Dates are very useful in bibliographical researches. *The Country Parson* and *Jacula Prudentum* were subsequently bound together with a new title-page as *Herbert's Remains*, 1652.

time, I beg of you to pray only the Litany, for I am weak and faint': and Mr. Duncon did so."

Again, it is remarkable that this work of "Proverbs" is not once mentioned by Barnabas Oley nor by Izaak Walton, in their biographies of Herbert; nor by Dr. Peckard in his enumeration of Herbert's works in *The Life of Nicholas Ferrar*, 1790, p. 208. The worthy angler, in his chit-chat with his piscatorial companions, frequently enlivened his discourse with a proverb or two, but on no occasion does he quote from those said to be selected by his much loved Herbert.

On the other hand, it is right to state that Herbert is said to have made a collection of Proverbs, for Mr. Mayor informs us, that in the Middle Hill MS. 9527, C. 8, is "a large book of stories, with outlandish proverbs at the end, Englished by Mr. George Herbert, in all 463 proverbs." (*Life of Nicholas Ferrar*, App., p. 302.) These proverbs, however, may have been copied from the printed book. But even with this statement before us, it is a matter deserving farther investigation, whether the work first published with his initials, without the imprimatur of any editor, and unnoted by his biographers, should be considered as indubitably the production of George Herbert.

J. YEOWELL.[1]

REPLIES—HERBERT'S "JACULA PRUDENTUM:" "FERRAR'S LIFE." (2ND S. ii. 88.)

The Middle Hill MS. (9527 C. art. 8., D. art. 3.) does not contain the "outlandish proverbs" at large, but merely a list of "Books and MSS. Belonging to [Ferrar's godson] Mr.

---

1 *Notes and Queries*, second series, Vol. 3, January–June, (London: Bell and Daley, 1857), p. 88–89.

John Mapletoft." In 1735, as I suppose, these MSS. were at Mr. Bunbury's of Great Catworth, where J. J. (whom I now know to have been John Jones of Welwyn [see Peckard's *Preface*, and Nichols' *Lit. Anecd.*, i. 638.]) appears to have seen them. He communicated an account of them to Peck. (See *Lives of Nicholas Ferrar*, Append., pp. 289 *n.*, 300–303.) Now we know from Mrs. Collett's letter to her son Edward (*Ibid.*, 313 *n.*) the high esteem in which Herbert's works were held at Gidding; and from Gidding Dr. John Mapletoft (afterwards the Gresham Professor) must have derived his two MS. collections of proverbs, one of which we know from Jones's catalogue professed to be a work of Herbert's. The arguments brought forward by MR. YEOWELL do not appear sufficient to shake the concurrent testimony of this Gidding MS., and of the title-pages of the first and second editions. For, 1. That the number of proverbs is greater in the second edition than in the first may be accounted for by supposing that the book was circulated (as indeed we know that it was) in MS. copies, and that the owners of copies considered themselves to be at liberty to add such proverbs as they met with from time to time. 2. The irregular paging of the second edition need not make us suspect foul play. Nothing is more common than such irregularities in books of that century: thus Hickman's *Historia Quinq-Articularis Exarticulata* (8vo., 1673, a curious book) runs on from 46 to 353. 3. Perhaps the "Prayers before and after Sermon" were intended for private use. Or if not, I see nothing in *The Country Parson*, or elsewhere, to prove that Herbert would scruple to use prayers of his own composition before and after sermon, and these prayers seem to be altogether in his tone. 4. Not even does Walton, much less do Oley or Peckard, profess to give a complete account of Herbert's works. 5. The erasure of the initials G. H. in the

Bodleian copy is the only argument for MR. YEOWELL's view which seems to me to be of weight. Perhaps other MS. notes may be found, which may help to clear up the difficulty.

From Herbert to Ferrar is but a step. Since I printed Jebb's *Life of Ferrar*, I have learnt that the "Dr. Jebb" whose name it bears was the well-known editor of *Aristides*, who was connected with the Cotton family. I have also obtained access to *The Christian's Magazine, or a Treasury of Divine Knowledge*, vol. ii., 1761, London, J. Newbery and J. Coote, in which several poems (chiefly translations) of Bishop Turner's are printed, and at p. 356. *seq.* his life of Ferrar. It is badly edited, some passages being curtailed, and some expressions altered for others of a newer mint; but enough is left to make it abundantly plain that Dr. Jebb merely retouched Turner's life. The two copies, however, supply one another's omissions, and may together enable us to reconstruct the original with some degree of probability. But I will not abandon the hope that John Ferrar's MS., or at least Peck's transcript of it, may yet be discovered, and make useless all the tasteless compilations which have rather obscured than illustrated the history of the Gidding family. Peckard tells us that most of Peck's papers passed into the hands of Sir Thomas Cave; and Chalmers says that Gilchrist possessed his *Life of Ferrar*. Where are they now, or where are the MSS. used by Peckard himself?

J. E. B. MAYOR.

ST. JOHN'S COLLEGE, CAMBRIDGE.[1]

WESTMINSTER REVIEW, JULY 1878, P. 126.

Every one will also gladly welcome Messrs. Rivingtons' handy

1 *Notes and Queries*, second series, Vol. 3, January–June, (London: Bell and Daley, 1857), p. 130–131.

edition of George Herbert.[1] Hitherto Herbert has been looked upon as the exclusive possession of the High Church party. Of late years, however, his popularity has very greatly widened. Secularists have been even patronising him. Emerson quotes from him oftener, perhaps, than from any other poet. It is noteworthy, too, that though Emerson in his "Parnassus" gives only two pieces, and both of them maimed and mangled, from Shelley, he quotes no less than sixteen from Herbert. We need not now inquire into the causes of Herbert's growing popularity. Two things, however, greatly contribute to it—his wide liberality, and a certain tendency to a vague kind of poetical mysticism. We are glad to see that Messrs. Rivington have republished the "Jacula Prudentium," which has been omitted in some recent editions. The collection is a curious one, and in many ways reflects the collector's mind. Of course, we must be prepared to find many proverbs from which we utterly disagree. Here, for instance, is one, which, taken in its literal sense, can only do more harm than good—"Every day brings its bread with it" (page 9). Unfortunately the mass of people will take sayings of this kind in their most literal sense. Our language is full of such proverbs, such as that most immoral one, "God never sends mouths with out sending bread to fill them." Here is another of the same type from George Herbert—"God sends cold according to clothes" (page 11), which is better known in its more modern form of "God tempers the wind to the shorn lamb," which is popularly supposed to occur somewhere in the Bible, but which Sterne stole from the French, translating "brabis" by "lamb" to give a more sentimental air, but only rendering the proverb doubly untrue, as nobody ever yet saw a shorn lamb. Herbert's collection, however, as we have

---

1 *The English Poems of George Herbert, Together with his Collection of Proverbs, entitled Jacula Prudentium*, (London: Rivington. 1878).

said, reflects his mind. There is a quaintness about many of the proverbs which is as delightful as some of the poet's own turns of thought; as, for instance, in the following, "truth and oil are ever above," which, for its pithiness, can only be equaled by the Latin adage, "love and a cough cannot be hid." Many of Herbert's proverbs, however, are often only translations from well-known Greek and Latin apophthegms. Thus, for instance, his proverb at page 62, "None is offended but by himself," is a seventeenth century version of the Stoic doctrine—*nemolœditur nisi à se ipso*, so often quoted by St. Chrysostom, and to which Bartley gave a new turn when he said, "no man is written down except by himself." "To offend," in the sense of to hurt, we need not say, is an Elizabethan phrase, employed more than once by Shakespeare. One or two of the proverbs, we may add, are somewhat differently quoted from the usual versions, and one or two slight misprints occur. For instance, we do not feel quite sure about the following at page 98, "A man of great memory without learning has a rock and a spindle, and no staff to spin." For "staff," we should probably read stuff, and then the sense is somewhat the same as in Joubert's reflection, "Les jeunes écrivains donnent à leur esprit beaucoup d'exercice et peu d'aliments."

———————

NOTES

MAN'S QUESTIONS & GOD'S ANSWERS

Am I accountable to God?
Each of us will give an account of himself to God. ROMANS 14:12 (NIV).

Has God seen all my ways?
Everything is uncovered and laid bare before the eyes of him to whom we must give account. HEBREWS 4:13 (NIV).

Does he charge me with sin?
But the Scripture declares that the whole world is a prisoner of sin. GALATIANS 3:22 (NIV).
All have sinned and fall short of the glory of God. ROMANS 3:23 (NIV).

Will he punish sin?
The soul who sins is the one who will die. EZEKIEL 18:4 (NIV).
For the wages of sin is death, but the gift of God is eternal life in Christ Jesus our Lord. ROMANS 6:23 (NIV).

Must I perish?
He is patient with you, not wanting anyone to perish, but everyone to come to repentance. 2 PETER 3:9 (NIV).

How can I escape?
Believe in the Lord Jesus, and you will be saved. ACTS 16:31 (NIV).

Is he able to save me?
Therefore he is able to save completely those who come to God through him. HEBREWS 7:25 (NIV).

Is he willing?
Christ Jesus came into the world to save sinners. 1 TIMOTHY 1:15 (NIV).

Am I saved on believing?
Whoever believes in the Son has eternal life, but whoever rejects the Son will not see life, for God's wrath remains on him. JOHN 3:36 (NIV).

Can I be saved now?
Now is the time of God's favor, now is the day of salvation. 2 CORINTHIANS 6:2 (NIV).

As I am?
Whoever comes to me I will never drive away. JOHN 6:37 (NIV).

Shall I not fall away?
Him who is able to keep you from falling. JUDE 1:24 (NIV).

If saved, how should I live?
Those who live should no longer live for themselves but for him who died for them and was raised again. 2 CORINTHIANS 5:15 (NIV).

What about death and eternity?
I am going there to prepare a place for you. I will come back and take you to be with me that you also may be where I am. JOHN 14:2-3 (NIV).

Made in the USA
Las Vegas, NV
13 December 2020